William R. Nicoll

The Incarnate Saviour

A life of Jesus Christ

William R. Nicoll

The Incarnate Saviour
A life of Jesus Christ

ISBN/EAN: 9783337314156

Printed in Europe, USA, Canada, Australia, Japan

Cover: Foto ©Lupo / pixelio.de

More available books at **www.hansebooks.com**

THE INCARNATE SAVIOUR

FROM REVIEWS AND OPINIONS OF

THE FIRST EDITION

The late Canon LIDDON.—"It commands my warm sympathy and admiration. I rejoice in the circulation of such a book, which I trust will be the widest possible."

Rev. Professor SANDAY, D.D.—"There was quite room for such a volume. It contains a great deal of thought, often penetrating and always delicate, and pleasingly expressed. The subject has been very carefully studied, and the treatment will, I believe, furnish much suggestive matter both to readers and preachers."

Baptist Magazine.—"A truly valuable contribution to the literature of 'the life of Christ.'"

Methodist Recorder.—"Cautiously and forcibly written — the production of a close thinker, and of a man who knows how to impress his thinkings upon others. It is a boon to the Church to have such a volume as this."

Evangelical Magazine.—"Singularly readable and admirably planned. It embraces a vast range of subjects, which are tersely, eloquently, and comprehensively treated."

THE
INCARNATE SAVIOUR

A LIFE OF JESUS CHRIST

BY THE REV.
W. ROBERTSON NICOLL, M.A., LL.D.
EDITOR OF "THE EXPOSITOR" "THE EXPOSITOR'S BIBLE"
ETC.

NEW AND CHEAPER EDITION

EDINBURGH
T. & T. CLARK, 38 GEORGE STREET
1897

PRINTED BY MORRISON AND GIBB LIMITED

FOR

T. & T. CLARK, EDINBURGH

LONDON: SIMPKIN, MARSHALL, HAMILTON, KENT, AND CO. LIMITED
NEW YORK: CHARLES SCRIBNER'S SONS
TORONTO: THE WILLARD TRACT DEPOSITORY

PREFACE TO NEW EDITION

IN the preface to the first edition of this little book I used the following words:—"Should this book meet with any acceptance, I hope at some future date to follow it with another on the 'Theology of Christ.' Many who in this age of unsettled opinions are unable to acquiesce in traditional systems, profess themselves ready to accept a theology which can fairly be made out from the life and teachings of Christ, apart from all other writings; and such might welcome an honest attempt to discover this." Circumstances prevented the fulfilment of this intention. But since then, as is well known, the subject has been pursued with great zest and ability. Unfortunately, as it seems to me, the main object of most books in which the study has been pursued, has been to disengage from the Gospels a purer Christianity than that which is presented in the New Testament as a whole. In other words, an attempt has been made to invalidate the teaching of the apostles. What I proposed was an attempt to show that the germs of the whole teaching of the Epistles were to be found in the words and works of Christ, taken as we find them in the four Gospels. As a rule, recent writers on the teaching of Jesus do not start from this basis. They do not accept the Gospels as they stand, but subject them to critical examination, and sift out the material they believe to be trustworthy. From this material they construe the teaching. They almost invariably glory in the fact that the result is different from the teaching found in the Epistles, and from the accepted doctrine of the Catholic Church.

(1) This process of winnowing is, no doubt, necessary from their point of view. The results, however, vary, as might be expected. An extreme writer like Havet does not even see any evidence that Jesus asserted Himself to be the Messiah, or made special enemies of the Pharisees, or denounced them in the words attributed to Him in the Gospels. All these assertions, as we find them in the Gospels now, were incorporated by a later generation; in fact, Havet excises so freely, that in the end he says that so little remains that it may be said to be "the soul of Jesus that escapes us." Others, who do not go nearly so far, apply subjective tests, and obtain a result that satisfies them by a liberal use of the knife to passages that controvert their opinions. Yet they strongly object to subjective reasoning on the other side. Take, for example, those passages in the Fourth Gospel, that have touched as no other words have ever done the very heart of Christendom, and see how they are treated. Yet it is with these chapters in view, that men unconsciously argue—"If these are not the words of Jesus, then a greater than Jesus is here."

Preface

(2) It is necessary to consider the relation of Christ's Word to His work. Did He come primarily to deliver a message to the world, or did He come in order that there might be a message to be delivered? Is the centre of His manifestation to be found in the gracious words that proceeded out of His mouth, or in His dying for the world that He might take its sins away?

(3) Admitting, as many will not admit, that our Lord spoke the promise of the Holy Ghost, was that promise fulfilled to the apostles, or was it not? If it was fulfilled to the apostles, all the questions about the relation between apostolic teaching and the teaching of our Lord become strangely irrelevant, if not even positively blasphemous. For the apostles claimed not to be delivering their own message, but to possess the mind of Christ. They claimed to be witnesses of Christ, and to have received the Holy Ghost. The Holy Ghost, according to the promise of Jesus, had led them into all the truth. Jesus Himself, through His Holy Spirit, had interpreted His life and death, and though they had known Christ after the flesh, yet from henceforth they knew Him so no more. To them He was the Lord of Glory. They were in direct communication with Him, and therefore their words revealed Christ. Their words were the continuation and completion of the Gospels. And so it has been steadfastly held that Christianity is what our Lord delivered to the apostles, and what the apostles delivered to the Church. If this is not so, then how has Christ's promise of the Spirit been fulfilled?

(4) It might be answered that essentially the message of the apostles is the message of Christ, but that in their words there is a larger element of weakness and fallibility; or it might even be said that in Christ's words there was no such element as existed in theirs. But the real question is not whether in every detail of their letters the apostles were right, but whether they were right in the great doctrines with which the Epistles are threaded through and through, as a leaf is threaded by its fibres. If these doctrines are true, and heartily accepted as the mind of Christ, there is very little to argue about. If they are not true, then the apostles corrupted Christianity. And this is the view to which much teaching of the present day is drifting.

(5) Is it possible to maintain, in view of the conditions of the Incarnation, that the words spoken by our Lord in the flesh are so incomparably raised above the words He afterwards spoke by His Holy Spirit, that the former cannot be placed on the same platform with the later? Some writers are to be commended so far for their sense of the supremacy of Jesus—a feeling which has led one or two of them to reject the doctrine of the Kenosis in every form. When they come to what seems incongruous with their conception of Christ, they are apt to pass it by as no part of the original tradition. But does the criticism which impugns the authority of the apostles stop short at last of impugning the authority of Christ? By such a writer as M. Havet we find Christ accused of severity and harshness, of

violence and imperiousness, of chagrin and bitter melancholy. We find it said that the faith of Jesus was a very narrow one, that He was no thinker, that He never brought light to dissipate the shadow, that He was simply a Jew ordained and exalted, "born in a country which nourished an independent and undocile spirit; one who obeyed His own inspirations more willingly than He obeyed authority; a man of nature rather than of the schools, made to compromise the Sanhedrin of Jerusalem and to ruin Himself, but made also to move the souls of men."

It will be seen, I venture to think, as time goes on, that the exaltation of the Christianity of the Gospels above that of the Epistles is ultimately fatal to Christianity in every form. As Dr. Denney says: "It is only in the Church that the Gospels have ever been appreciated or understood, and they have never been appreciated or understood as in any kind of rivalry or contrast to the New Testament revelation of Christ as a whole. The Spirit which created and which lives in the Church, reveals Christ in Gospel and Epistle alike, and without this revelation the Gospels themselves, the very words of Jesus, reveal nothing."

HAMPSTEAD, *September* 1897.

"Many soul longings
 Have I had in my day.
 Now the hope of my life
 Is that tree of triumph,
 Ever to turn to.
 Mighty my will is
 To cleave to the Crucified;
 My claim for shelter
 Is—right to the Rood."
    CÆDMON'S *Cross Lay.*

CONTENTS

CHAP.		PAGE
	INTRODUCTION	1
I.	The Birth and Infancy of Christ	9
II.	Jesus as a Child	23
III.	The Silent Years of Jesus	37
IV.	John Baptist and the Baptism of Christ	51
V.	The Temptation of Christ	65
VI.	The Object and Claims of Christ	79
VII.	The Miracles of Christ	91
VIII.	The Teaching of Christ	111
IX.	The Apostles of Christ	125
X.	Christ's Intercourse with God	137
XI.	Christ dealing with Inquirers	153
XII.	Christ's Replies to His Enemies	169
XIII.	Christ's Toil for Men	179
XIV.	The Transfiguration of Christ	191
XV.	The Prevision of the Cross	203
XVI.	Judas Iscariot	215
XVII.	Gethsemane	227
XVIII.	The Trial of Christ	239

Contents

CHAP.		PAGE
XIX.	The Seven Words on the Cross	253
XX.	The Burial and Resurrection of Christ	267
XXI.	The Resurrection Life of Christ	283
XXII.	The Ascension of Christ	295
XXIII.	The Character of Christ	307
	Notes	319

THE INCARNATE SAVIOUR

INTRODUCTION

ALTHOUGH it is true that there will always be fresh occasion for writing the life of Christ, the subject being exhaustless, and the ceaseless gravitation of human thought thereto one of the most impressive proofs of the divinity of the original, yet I should not have thought of writing this book merely as another narration and grouping of the outward facts. The scenery of Palestine, the customs of the changeless East, the idioms of Oriental speech, the literary phenomena of the gospel history, and the modes of contemporary thought,—these have been set forth lately with the highest skill and learning. There is a place, doubtless, for all these things, for Jesus Christ belongs to human history. But He is living still, and the events of His life are not separated from us by eighteen hundred years of the sorrowful experiences of humanity. While they have their place in time, they yet transcend it, and are of everlasting significance. To that inward significance we turn our thoughts in the following pages, and it was at first designed to call the volume "The Inner Life of Christ." The objection to this was, that the inner life of Christ cannot be satisfactorily treated of without to a certain extent narrating its outward course. But the narrative here will not be sufficient for those who are not already familiar with it. It is given only in so far as it seems to bear upon the propositions which this work aims to illustrate. Before the life of Christ there is prophecy, and after it explanation,—both prophecy and explanation being inspired. At present we do not deal directly either with what goes before or comes after; but it is believed that the propositions advanced are in harmony with the words of prophets and apostles.

We endeavour to illustrate three main propositions in the following pages. First, Jesus Christ was God and man in two distinct natures and one person. His humanity was true and proper, but through it we see continually gleams of the Godhead. As the Apostle John says in the preface to his Gospel, "The Word was made flesh, and dwelt among us, *and we beheld His glory*." This glory, as we understand the words, was not merely beheld by the apostle in such great and signal manifestations as the transfiguration, the resurrection, and the ascension,—it was beheld more or less clearly even in the lowly actions and the ordinary tenor of His common life and speech. For example, we are told that after one of His miracles the disciples put the question, "What manner of man is this?" That He was a man they never doubted, yet ever and anon there was something which suggested He was more. The look in His face, the tone in His voice, the work of His hands, constantly startled them,

—made their hearts burn, and called them to reverence and homage. He was near them, and yet there was an infinite separateness; between the last touch of familiarity and Himself, a look, a tone parted them. When they began to feel almost on a level with Him, some question would humble them, and open the depths of their ignorance; some word coming out of eternity made them wonder if, after all, He was the son of Joseph. To use a familiar illustration,—A company of men are gathered together talking without restraint, and amongst them one higher than themselves is introduced disguised. The disguise outwardly is complete, and for a time undetected. It is not long, however, before it is penetrated. And what discovers it is little —a tone, a glance may be enough. Even this might prompt the question, "<u>What manner of man is this?</u>"

We shall find illustrations innumerable as we proceed. In His first miracle He made wine, and yet it was not the wine which other men made; neither was it made after their measure. The master of the feast, mistakenly speaking to the bridegroom, gave all unconsciously the true keynote to the life of Christ, when he said, Every man—but thou. Every man—that is one side, that is the way of humanity; but thou— everything that thou doest, though the same, is yet infinitely different. And to take one incident from the end, we read that before His death He washed the disciples' feet. He took the towel, and stooped low to this mean act of service. But side by side with this humbling of Himself we see the light of His divine glory, for He took the towel knowing that He was from God, and going to God. In the supreme exaltation of His consciousness of divinity He bent to lowly service, and thus glorified it for ever; and, were our discernment deep and clear enough, we should see about every act Christ did, and every word Christ spoke, some mark of divinity, some subtle property that does not and cannot belong to man. We go over the beautiful story of His humanity, saying at every point, "Lo! this is our God; we have waited for Him, and He will save us." Only our blindness will keep us from seeing in every incident, in every word, the broad arrow of the kingdom of heaven, the image and superscription of the Son of God.

Secondly, we further aim at showing that Jesus Christ came to suffer in order that He might save. His life did not begin at Bethlehem,—He was from eternity. He came into the world with His life-plan foretold, and moved in obedience to old and sacred words of prophecy. His purpose did not gradually lay hold of Him,—it was a complete thought from the first. Many men grope from littleness step by step into greatness; but He came into the world with a plan He never amended. To us each day comes as a new surprise, and we are at the mercy of events. To Him nothing came suddenly, and all the seemingly unrelated events of His life go together to form one vast unity. We see this most impressively when we consider that He came to die. Other men have their lives interrupted by death,—other men begin their careers of reform with hopes of victory and coronation, and though death often comes to destroy their hopes, it is a death all undreamt of in their earlier hours.

INTRODUCTION

But to this man death, though it came with all the accompaniments of horror, was not a surprise nor an interruption, but the very work which He came into the world to do. He <u>foretold</u> His own death in all its circumstances. The statement may be passed over unthinkingly, but the more we ponder it, the more its mystery will grow upon us. It is the tritest of commonplaces that no man knows the day of his own death. Even when it is clear that life is near its close, the most experienced skill will be baffled in trying to foretell the hour of its end. What shall we say of Him who from the beginning saw clear before Him that cross upon which He was to be lifted up, and who, instead of mourning over that cross as the symbol of the extinction and defeat of all His hopes and works, gloried in it as the sign under which He was to conquer and to lead His followers on to victory.

We shall show in the following pages how the shadow of this cross lies over all His life,—how it is impossible to understand that life apart from it,—how it touches the very cradle of His childhood, and is never anywhere absent,—how His whole progress through life is a progress to the cross. "Where," runs an old Rabbinical saying,—"where is the true Messiah to be found? Sitting at the gate of Rome" (the symbol of the Gentile world) "among the lepers, binding and bandaging His wounds." The sign-manual of the Messiah is that He should suffer.

Thirdly, we endeavour to show the sweet and perfect accord of Christ's words, works, and thoughts. We take His teaching, and ask whether He lived as

He preached. We take His works, and ask whether they were the mere tricks and feats of a deft conjurer, or whether they were true expressions of His soul. We follow Him into the solitude of the mountain, the silence of the garden, the hush of the upper chamber, and listen to His communings with God. We watch all His words, and mark those rare and precious revealings of His inner nature, which come from Him now in a strain of sorrow, and again in the confidence of sympathy. Into these windows we gaze to see the working of His heart. Most reverently, yet most jealously, we scrutinise all, and we come to see in the end that all is of one piece. Every other life has notes that ring harshly. Every disguise men have ever worn has sometimes slipped off; every mask has sometimes shown the truth behind it. But He could have worn no disguise, for with all our scrutiny we must confess that we cannot convince Him of sin, and that only one key will open the lock of His life. In other words, what He was in any one place at any one time, He was always and everywhere; so that, though the mirror of the gospel history be broken in a thousand fragments, every fragment yields the same image of the God-man, the Redeemer of the world.

These points, though not minutely insisted upon, have been borne in mind all through; and although this book assumes the truth of the gospel history, and is thus not directly addressed to unbelievers, yet there is an argument, and that of the most weighty kind, contained in the very harmony and simplicity of the character traced in it. Whence came he? What imagination gave Him birth? Did He rise out of the disharmony of a Jewish peasant household? Was He the product of that Eastern soil? or was He what He claimed to be? Those who do not admit the true doctrine of His person and work, are continually brought to a standstill by astonishment. We, too, marvel, but with us the mysteries are not many. They have been reduced to one,—God was manifest in the flesh. "Rabbi, thou art the Son of God; Rabbi, thou art the King of Israel."

I
THE BIRTH AND INFANCY OF CHRIST

"Unto us a Child is born; unto us a Son is given."

" A child He was, and had not learned to speak,
Who with His words the world before did make;
His mother's arms Him bare, He was so weak,
Who with His hands the vault of heaven could shake.
See how small room my infant Lord doth take,
Whom all the world is not enough to hold;
Who of His years as of His age hath told,
Never such age so young, never a child so old."

GILES FLETCHER.

CHAPTER I

THE BIRTH AND INFANCY OF CHRIST

A VILLAGE maiden, of whose previous history we know almost nothing, had the homely tenor of her life one day strangely broken by the descent of the angel Gabriel, and his salutation, "Hail, thou that art highly favoured, the Lord is with thee: blessed art thou among women." In the midst of her troubled surmisings as to what the meaning of this salutation might be, he announced to her that she was to bear the promised Messiah. She was thus called to the most awful charge ever laid upon a mortal creature. The call was as overwhelming as it was sudden and startling. From the privacy of her obscure life, she was summoned to be the instrument of the fulfilment of God's greatest purpose and the accomplishment of God's most amazing work. She was to be the last link in the long chain of chosen souls through whom God's purpose had advanced, and in her it was to be consummated. In her, man and God were to be brought into the most inexpressible closeness. She was to be the human mother of the eternal Son.[1] What consequences were to be involved in this election none could dream; only,

[1] See Church's *Human Life*, p. 172.

as the call was great, there must be much to endure, to surrender, to anticipate. It is idle to try to imagine what the state of the soul of the maiden must have been when she heard of the place she was to fill in the eternal plan. What tides of fear and rapture, of shame and wonder, swept through the gentle heart we cannot even dream; but her answer was one of profound and humble obedience. She was betrothed to Joseph, and standing on the brink of a new life at a time when, if ever, the heart flutters on widespread wings of hope and fear, and excited words rush to the lips; but before the holy angel, and with her heart filled by his great message, there was neither dejection nor exultation. He came and went, and she remained in her sweet humility waiting the fulfilment of the word of the Lord. That her character was singularly pure, simple, and religious, is quite apparent. The very fact of her being chosen to be the mother of the Messiah, is proof in itself of that. But it appears also from the unconsciousness and the gentle greatness of trust with which she accepted the overwhelming honour that was put upon her. In the thought of God's presence with her, in the thought of accomplishing His purpose, all hopes and fears and loves of her own little life went clean out of sight. The Lord had magnified her, she was His handmaid; He might do with her in all things as He willed.

We read next of her going to Elizabeth, who was soon to obtain the dearest wish of a Jewish woman, in having a son. When she stood on the threshold of her kinswoman's house, she was received by a joyful salutation, which confirmed to her the angel's message.

Elizabeth's words of blessing went beyond those of the angel. Being filled with the Holy Ghost, she said, "Blessed art thou among women, and blessed is the fruit of thy womb." Thus the angel's message was confirmed by human voice. What she had hidden in the deep silence of her trustful heart, what she had believed, and yet trembled to believe, was made real by another, and that repressed still spirit broke forth in words of song, in which she poured out her praise to God who had shown His mercy to the humble. "All generations," she sings in her gladness, "shall call me blessed,"—a true woman's thought of happiness— blessedness in blessing others. Her song is the last word of the old covenant and the opening utterance of the gospel. While retaining the form and colour of the old Hebrew poetry, it quivers tremulously with the great and partially disclosed revelation about to be given. The hymn, like others that stand near it, could not have been sung earlier or later. "Such sunlit mountain-tops in the distance, with such mists over the paths that lead to them, such a firm grasp of salvation and redemption, such a clear view of its character, and such silence as to its details, can only belong to the thin border line of a period neither quite Jewish nor quite Christian. A little less, and these songs would be purely Jewish; a little more, and they would be purely Christian."[1] After this song was sung, she returned to feel the beginning of the pain and sorrow that were to come along with the great honour which was hers by the divine election. Joseph was minded to

---

[1] See Bishop Alexander's *Leading Ideas of the Gospels*, p. 107; and Mill's *Pantheistic Theories of the Gospels*.

put her away privily. Angels in heaven, sisters on earth, had been singing her praise, and how sharp the contrast must have been of the suspicion under which she now fell of vulgar sin! The very tenderness of her betrothed husband must have made the wound sharper, but whatever that wound was, we hear nothing of it. She yielded herself to the stream of the divine will, and was guided on by the current, nor did she depart at all from the spirit in which she first received her commission: "Behold the handmaid of the Lord; be it unto me according to Thy word."

Her child was conceived of the Holy Ghost. "A virgin," it had been written of old, shall conceive and bear a son." This miraculous conception must form the beginning of any true estimate of the life of Christ. Either it is fact or falsehood. If it be falsehood, let it be utterly repudiated as a baseless and blasphemous superstition; if it be truth, let us recognise it as a truth of such importance that it is quite idle to study the life of Christ without taking it into constant account. For, first, it signifies that Jesus Christ was more than man. He was the child of the Holy Ghost. His pedigree is given to us, and in the long line of his ancestors we mark the famous, the unknown, the infamous, bright and dark commingled, but none of all escaped the universal taint of sin. For all those years the tyrannical tradition of evil had never been broken. The sin of our first parents had passed on from generation to generation, and each of the millions of mankind had to say, "Behold, I was shapen in iniquity, and in sin did my mother conceive me." Each fulfilled in his life all too truly the sad promise of his birth. How was this tradition to be broken, and yet broken by one who really belonged to the race? The instinct of man has foreshadowed the truth. Stories of a virgin birth, here and there discernible in Paganism, show the deep intuition of the human race which was realised in Christ. He came into the world to fight with sin; He came to redeem a race steeped in a terrible heritage of evil, and that He might redeem them He Himself was free from the evil. Besides, His immaculate conception points to the fact that He did not come into being then, but that He was merely manifested. He had existed from eternity, and now entered into the sphere of sense and time. How could the entrance of such a being be marked? It was marked by the suspension of the law of nature. He entered into the world a true man, and yet by a way never used before or since.

Again, this child was born into the world with a distinct mission. Before He came He was named by the angel, "Jesus." His name was called Jesus, because He was to save His people from their sins. When He lay in the cradle His destiny was written upon His brow. Other children are mysterious enigmas, to be solved by the progress of time. It is a bold thing to foretell any child's future. Children of the rich have died poor; children of many prayers have become earthly, sensual, devilish. But this child was born to fight with sin, and to conquer it. All that He spoke, all that He did, was to relate to sin. He thus challenges our intensest scrutiny from the first; and, knowing the issues that depend on His behaviour, we may well gaze on it with an agony of earnestness. For He must not only come untainted into the world, but, from the time He draws His first breath to the hour when He commends His spirit to the Father, He must resist every assault, escape every pollution of evil. One evil thought dimming but for an instant the crystal clearness of His soul, and all is lost. The Saviour from sin must be in all battles, great and small, the conqueror of sin.

We read that Joseph and Mary were summoned, by an edict of the Emperor Augustus, to travel the hundred miles that lay between Nazareth and Bethlehem, to register their names. Though peasants, they were of the city of David, and belonged to Bethlehem. When they reached the inn, after their long journey, they found it crowded, and were fain to take refuge in a corner of the inn yard that would otherwise have been occupied by beasts. At the period of her life when even poverty strains itself to provide its utmost of comfort and even luxury, in her hour of trial, in the midst of strangers, and without womanly hand to help her, the virgin mother brought forth her first-born son, and wrapped him in swaddling-clothes, and laid him in a manger, because there was no room for them in the inn. The noise and bustle of the world surged on around them, and none but Joseph and Mary knew that the Messiah, the Saviour of the world, had been born of the carpenter's bride.

But the revelation was soon given from heaven, and given to some humble, simple souls, spiritually akin to the virgin. The angels told the glad tidings of great joy to a company of shepherds on the plains of Bethle-

THE BIRTH AND INFANCY OF CHRIST

hem: "Unto you is born this day, in the city of David, a Saviour, which is Christ the Lord. And this shall be the sign unto you; You shall find him wrapped in swaddling-clothes, and lying in a manger." The deep token of the divine presence was not a glory in earth or heaven,—for God's thoughts are not as our thoughts, —it was a helpless babe and a manger cradle. Nor is this out of analogy with the rest of His life. He came to identify Himself with the race of simple, fallen, straying men. He came to put on our nature, not in its ornaments or embellishments of rank, or wealth, or culture, but as it was in its poorest and humblest experience and conditions. So it was fit that He should come in such a fashion that none are poorer, none humbler, none less noble after the flesh than He. The earthly conditions were of the lowliest. It was the mark of the Messiah that they should be so; yet through all the lowliness the glory shines.

For to that humble cradle and that young child there came not the shepherds alone. It had been foretold that kings should come to the brightness of His rising, and this word was fulfilled in the coming of the wise men from the East. They toiled across the desert to adore Him. Their homes were probably in Parthia, and they belonged to the caste of Magi, who represented the wisdom of the Eastern world. They were looking for a deliverer, as men were at the time, from the East, and, like all sincere and humble seekers, they were favoured with divine guidance. They were led across the long space by a star, which they gazed at and followed day by day and night by night, till at length they found themselves in the sacred city Jerusalem. From Jerusalem they were guided to Bethlehem by a star, which went before them till it came and stood where the young child was. In their trustful simplicity they were not repelled by the apparent lowliness of the King. They believed in Him and worshipped Him, and gave gold, frankincense, and myrrh. They fell down, not examining their Lord curiously as an intellectual puzzle, but feeling that they had reached in Him the very centre and source of being. He had come, not only to be the glory of His people Israel, but to be a light to lighten the Gentiles, and these Gentiles who came to Him in His cradle were first of all the long line of the nations that were to receive His illumination.

These righteous, waiting souls are the type of those who, true to the light they have, and seeking more, are not denied the boon. Like Cornelius and the eunuch of Ethiopia, they were, as it has been phrased, flowing gently along in the channel where they were overtaken by the waters of grace.[1] Those who follow the lights, the stars, of God, find that they brighten, and do not cease till they have guided to the Sun.

They are also a type of the kings, not of earthly descent only, but as well of mind and heart, who are drawn to Christ. Jesus Christ is the true "Master of those who know"; and if He has found many of His best and steadiest friends amongst the humble, as He did among the shepherds, He has drawn also from the wisest and the most noble. Poetry, eloquence, learning, have been devoted to His service; nor has He missed some tribute of the precious things of the earth.

[1] J. E. B. in *The Patience of Hope*.

The gold, frankincense, and myrrh, and more especially the undoubting, simple worship, were a grateful earnest of the offerings to be.

On the eighth day after His birth He was circumcised,—made under the law, entering into the covenant, and having His name inscribed in the roll of the nation. Soon after, He was taken to the Temple. There was nothing to a superficial observer in the sight; but when the Lord of the Temple suddenly came to His house, He did not miss a welcome. Poor people have brought the offering of pigeons and doves. An old man and woman, who seem to have overpassed the period of useful service, and to be fit only for death, come forward to receive Him. This is all the world sees, and it negligently passes on. But to the eye of faith there is here the coming of the rightful heir, in disguise of a stranger, to visit His own house; and His aged saints have been waiting long to receive Him. Simeon, the aged man, had received the promise that he should not see death till he had seen the Lord's Christ. If he received the promise early, what a strange, charmed, expectant life he must have led! He could not die, no matter what danger threatened, till Christ had been seen. But the years passed, and his hair grew white, and his step tottered as he entered the Temple, and his companions dropped at his side, and he wondered why he was so long kept out of heaven.[1] Anna, the prophetess, had dwelt in the Temple nearly all her long life, departing not from it night nor day. One thing

---

[1] It is a fair inference from the narrative that Simeon was an aged man.

she had desired of the Lord, that did she seek after, that she might dwell in the house of the Lord all the days of her life, to behold the beauty of the Lord, and to inquire in His Temple; and she did behold the beauty of the Lord at last, when the young child was carried in. It was revealed to the aged pair that this was the Messiah, and they lifted up their voices in praise, and felt that now they had nothing to do but die. Happy souls that saw Him thus, and passed away before the years of trial came!—happy souls, whose dream was not broken by the storm and tragedy of His later life! Taught by the Spirit, they may have had a deeper and truer fore-glimpse of Christ than many; yet to foresee and to bear are different things, even when the sight is clearest; and they may well be counted happy, who, with the assurance that Christ was come, and fresh from the joy of holding Him, fell asleep, "spared the trial of finding Him at last unfold to a form at variance with their dream." Others were to live, and the sword was to pierce their hearts: *they* died unwounded.

"A sword," said Simeon, speaking by the Holy Ghost to the young mother, "shall pierce through thy own soul also." It was not long before she felt its keenness. Herod, the prince of the country, then in his old age, tortured with disease and remorse, had heard that Jesus was born, and sought to find from the Magi where He was. Warned of God in a dream, they did not return to tell him, and in his fury he sent his soldiers to murder the babes in Bethlehem, but Jesus was gone. He had been taken down into

Egypt by the command of God, to be there until the danger was over.

We see already, then, the mingled humility and greatness of Christ, His Godhead, and His manhood; we see already the shadow of the cross lying over the cradle. We see Him set for the fall as well as for the rising of men, and for a sign that shall be spoken against. He comes into the world as God emptied of His glory so far as that could be, and yet with His divinity clearly manifested. The wise men adore Him; He has to flee into Egypt. He comes to suffer, and the suffering begins with His life. The chastisement of our peace is upon Him from the very first.

The flight to Egypt not only saved Him from the murderous malice of Herod, but also served to secure the true human development of His life. If He had remained in an atmosphere of portent and wonder, a true natural growth would have been impossible; but by this break, whatever there was of wonder or surmise had time to die down, and, when Joseph after Herod's death returned to dwell at Nazareth, all was forgotten, and He grew up in the humble home as the child of the carpenter and his wife.[1]

This is not the mere history of the past; it touches us livingly. A mediæval preacher[2] begins a sermon from the text, "Unto us a Child is born; unto us a Son is given":—"And thus it is that we know Him to be born, because He is given. For His birth would avail us nothing unless He were also our own; and He would in vain be made the Son of man unless it were given to us to become the sons of God. Behold how

[1] See Note A.   [2] Guaric.

Jesus is offered to us; hasten to meet Him; stretch forth your hands, make ready your affections, prove your devotion by acts as well as words." The kingdom of heaven could not be set up among men without affecting profoundly and radically their whole circumstances. Since He came, and spoke, and died, the world has had to reckon with a new agent, that is to disturb as well as calm, to cast down as well as raise. Joseph and Mary are disquieted; Herod trembles on his throne; the babes of Bethlehem die, and the air is rent with their mothers' cries. Such are the prefigurations of the revolution made in the world by the coming of Jesus Christ.

II
JESUS AS A CHILD

"I have more understanding than all my teachers, for thy testimonies are my meditation. I understand more than the ancients, because I keep thy precepts."

                              "Good father,
Which of the angels do they miss in heaven?
Ofttimes at mass I press him close, and tremble,
To the sweet voices, lest at 'in excelsis'
He should remember, and go back."
                                      SYDNEY DOBELL.

CHAPTER II

JESUS AS A CHILD

THE records of Christ's childhood are tantalisingly brief, and the efforts which have been made to supplement them are useful mainly as a foil to them, showing how unequal is the human imagination to such a task. Jesus grew up in a humble home. He shared the lot of His reputed father Joseph and His mother Mary. They dwelt in Nazareth, an obscure and petty village, inhabited by a wild and rough people. We have already traced faintly the beauties of the character of Mary, and Joseph in his humility and righteousness was a fit husband to such a wife. There were other inmates in the home,—Jesus had brothers and sisters. He grew up, therefore, under the most healthy influences. In a soft atmosphere of love He received the nurture and admonition of the Lord. He was not learned,—not a proficient in the studies of the Scribes. But the Old Testament was familiar to Him; He knew it in Hebrew, as we find from His after quotations. The language which He spoke was either Aramaic, a provincial and north country dialect, or Greek, the language of education, and the vehicle of the greatest uninspired thought of the world. And although Nazareth was so little favoured in its inhabitants, it was a place favoured with the choicest influences of nature. There is no place in Palestine even yet that is haunted by flowers as Nazareth is. It lies in a dell surrounded by hills, and one hill, of some five hundred feet high above the village, gives one of the most magnificent spectacles in the world,—a spectacle on which the eyes of Jesus must often have rested with rapture. We may suppose also that Joseph taught his reputed son the rudiments of his trade, and thus the quiet years wore on.

Jesus Christ might have come into the world as a man full grown, but He condescended to come as a child, and to undergo the endearing changes by which the infant passes into a child, the child into a youth, and the youth into a man. There was in Him a changeless element that was divinely faultless, but there was also a changing element by which He was developed. As has been remarked, we have no stories of His precocity, and the imagination of man has failed to conceive any that can be accepted as even possible. An acute thinker has observed that our anxiety to have anecdotes of the childhood of great men, rises from our desire to be confirmed in the belief that great achievements come from great gifts, and are not possible except to those who have been exceptionally endowed from the beginning. However that may be, we are told nothing of the childhood of Jesus, save the incident we are now to consider. He grew in knowledge, His knowledge not being of many books, but of one book.

He also grew in wisdom, a very different thing from knowledge.

> "Knowledge and wisdom, far from being one,
> Have ofttimes no connection: knowledge dwells
> In heads replete with thoughts of other men;
> Wisdom in minds attentive to their own.
> Knowledge,—a rude, unprofitable mass,
> The mere materials with which wisdom builds,—
> Till smoothed and squared, and fitted to its place,
> Does but encumber when it should enrich.
> Knowledge is proud that he has learned so much;
> Wisdom is humble that he knows no more." [1]

Thus the days passed, and found Him increasingly in favour with God and man.

When He was twelve years of age, the sole recorded incident of His childhood occurred. His parents went up to the Temple. They left their homes to go to Jerusalem and offer the paschal sacrifice. They had no fear to leave all behind, for enemies were kept from the land while they were away. Neither were they afraid of Archelaus, in spite of the memories of the murderous intent of Herod. They resolved to go, and to take Jesus with them. Women were not actually bound to go, but devout women like Hannah and Mary would count it a privilege and not a burden, and would be all the more willing to render the service because it was not actually enjoined.

We can perhaps conceive something of the feelings of Jesus in view of the feast. He had been brought up in that humble village; His view of human nature, although clear, would be restricted, and there would be

[1] Cowper.

in Him a noble curiosity to see human life in a great centre. His mind was just opening, far from being dulled as yet to the wonders and the great surprises of living; and we may conceive how this child would anticipate the sight of men,—the sight of places with whose history He had been long familiar, and, above all, the sight of that Temple which was the house of God. At twelve, like other Jewish boys at the same age, He entered on a new division of life. He became a child of the precept, and, after being examined in the sacred books, was bound to a man's obedience of the law.

We are able to follow the pilgrims in imagination. Their road was haunted by wild beasts and banditti. For defence they kept together, and as they journeyed they sang, their songs being probably the fifteen psalms after the 119th. They would sing among the Arab tribes, "Woe is me that I sojourn in Mesech, and dwell in the tents of Kedar." When they escaped the troops of their foes, they would sing, "My soul has escaped as a bird out of the snare of the fowler." When they were journeying in cheerful accord, they sang, "Behold how good and pleasant a thing it is for brethren to dwell together in unity." Jesus would take part in the songs, and understand their meaning; and we can imagine how His soul was thrilled with memories, when He saw the Jordan and those other scenes that made the stories on which His childhood had been nourished so real. But, above all, when Jerusalem came in sight, and the pilgrims shouted, "I will lift up mine eyes to the hills whence my help cometh"—when the mass of the great Temple, white on its uplifted rock, fell upon His eyes, what must His feelings have been! Never was any city of earth loved so dearly as Jerusalem, whose name is thus fitly applied to the city on high, which is the mother of us all. And when He arrived at Jerusalem, He would not merely be impressed by the natural sights, but He would feel His soul drawn out by the sight of the great multitude of different countries who thronged the streets of the city. Hundreds of other nations had become proselytes to the Jewish religion, and were gathered there to render homage to the one God. How would the Son of man feel, beholding for the first time this realisation, broken and imperfect though it was, of the unity of humanity in God! How must He feel in the consciousness that in Him the sundered hearts were to be gathered into one!

In Jerusalem, some who came up to keep the Passover were accommodated in private houses, and paid as the price of the accommodation, the skin of the lamb and the utensils they employed in cooking. Often, however, every place being crowded, they had to dwell in tents outside the walls of the city. If so, Joseph would have gone probably with Jesus to the Temple to kill his Passover lamb. Jesus would see the blood gushing into the golden cup, and thrown at the foot of the altar of burnt-offering. Then came the return to the tent with the carcase of the lamb and the preparation of supper, at which at least ten people had to be present. First the lamb was roasted, being thrust through with skewers of pomegranate wood, and then put into the midst of a red-hot oven. Afterwards would be placed near at hand a plate of unleavened bread, another of bitter herbs, and a vessel containing a thick sauce made like clay, to remind them of the brick-making in Egypt. Before the lamb was eaten, Joseph would take the cup of red wine, of which all drank. The lamb was then placed before him. The second cup of wine was filled, and some child—it might have been Jesus—asked the head of the house, "What mean ye by this service?" The story was then told of the deliverance from Egypt. The bitter herbs were a remembrance of the bitter bondage, and the unleavened bread of the haste in which the nation was thrust out. The 113th and the 114th Psalms were then sung. Then the lamb was carved and eaten. Wine was partaken of once more, and the 115th, 117th, and 118th Psalms were then sung. What must the Lamb of God have felt, listening and looking on in the presence of all this!

When all was accomplished, and they had returned home, it was found that Jesus was lost. It was customary for all the men to travel by themselves in one company, and all the women in another, the boys travelling either with father or mother. This may explain why He was lost. Or it may be explained by supposing that such confidence was put in Him, that it was not thought needful to seek Him, or be troubled about His absence at first. He had gone to the Temple, and was found there among the doctors, both hearing and asking them questions. It was not wonderful that He should be there. The seven days of the paschal feast were not enough for Him. He began to burn with that zeal for God's house which afterwards consumed Him. One day in these courts was better than all the thousands that had gone by in Nazareth. He was led to the Temple by His love for knowledge, and made acquaintance there with the great movements of thought. Ideas existing in germ burst then into flower. We need not suppose that there was sudden and disturbing development. The child grew, and the language in which He speaks to His father and mother is not that which would follow upon a sudden thought, but rather upon one long familiar. But He would learn in the Temple not merely from the words spoken, but by the sights He saw, and by the songs in His ears. The Temple music, the Temple service, would remind Him of His true home in heaven, where praises arise continually, and where worship is continually offered. The chord struck in His nature vibrated sweetly and solemnly. He felt that this, and not the cottage of the carpenter, was His Father's house.

The crises, if we may so call them, of the development of Christ's thoughts and plans, cannot, I think, be decided with the materials at our disposal. This much we may say with some confidence, that there was nothing to disturb His true humanity. We do not suppose that He became conscious in the Temple for the first time of His sonship and of His commission, for there is a tone of recollection in the words He speaks; and, besides, there would be something inconsistent with a normal development in so sudden and startling a revelation. Neither do we suppose that as a babe on His mother's breast He was conscious of all that He had come into the world to do, for that also would be to violate a true conception of His nature and of ordinary development. Nothing more can be said, than that He grew in wisdom and stature, and in favour with God and man; that the germ was there at the first, and steadily grew to its fulfilment.

His father and mother sought Him among His kinsfolk and acquaintance. Says Bishop Hall: "The parents of Christ knew him well to be of a disposition not strange, nor sullen and Stoical, but sweet and sociable; and therefore they supposed He had spent the time on the way in company of their friends and neighbours. They did not suspect Him wandered into the solitary fields, but when evening came they go to seek Him among their kinsfolk and acquaintance. If He had not wonted to converse formerly with them, He had not now been sought amongst them. Neither as God nor man does He take pleasure in a stern, froward austerity and wild retiredness, but in a mild affableness and amiable conversation." He was different from His kinsman John the Baptist, who was nourished in the desert till the day of his showing forth unto Israel. He grew up in the home—in the shop with His father, in the house with His mother, in the neighbours' cottages, winning their hearts—sweet and sociable as a child, even as He was when a man. We find Him in after life mixing freely with people of all classes and conditions, frequent alike in scenes of joy and sorrow, and the child was father to the man.

After three days they found Him. Even as He was lost three days at the end, so it was at the beginning. And He was found at last among the doctors. The pure and eager young face had been seen among the circle of the sages. He had been asking them questions, for He was anxious to learn. What kind of questions they were we may conjecture readily. He was asking them about the meaning of that word to whose mysteries they professed to have the key; but He was teaching them, waking new trains of thought, throwing new gleams of light among those old students; as it is written, "I have more understanding than all my teachers, for Thy testimonies are my meditation. I understand more than the ancients, because I keep Thy precepts." He had meditated, He had kept the word, and so those grey-bearded listeners were thunderstruck at His understanding and answers. "I have learned," said one, "much from the Rabbis my teachers; I have learned more from the Rabbis my colleagues; I have learned most of all from my disciples."[1] When His parents came in, the child would move to them, and it is noticeable that His mother speaks first. He belonged to her rather than to Joseph, and she says, "Why hast thou thus dealt with us? Thy father and I have sought thee sorrowing," or rather, "tormented." The sword of prophecy was again piercing her heart,— the sword that she had felt when she had to hasten with Him to Egypt, but whose sharpness she had time in those tranquil years to forget. She feels it in all its keenness: they were tormented, tortured with anxiety. "How is it," He replies, "that ye sought me? Wist ye not that I must be in my Father's house?" There is no regret, not even sympathy with their anxiety, but rather a mild rebuke that they did not know, as they might have done, where He was to be found. "Wist

[1] See Plumptre's *Christ and Christendom*, p. 100.

ye not that I must be in my Father's house?"[1]—a gentle reminder also that Joseph was not His father, but that God was. This question shows of what nature the unrecorded questions must have been. He says in effect, You might have known that I would not be found admiring the outward show, that I would not have sought the haunts of pleasure, that I would not have deserted you for any place but this. How early the keynote of His life was struck! How different was His childhood from other childhoods! What pathos there is in the thought that He took hold of realities so soon, having little space for laughter and for joys, and beginning His Father's work at twelve years of age! Of our childhood we may all say,

> " Unthinking, idle, wild, and young,
> I talked and laughed, and danced and sung."

But how soon the awful shadow fell upon His brow! And yet, although His parents did not understand Him, and although He had gained full comprehension of His destiny, He went down into Nazareth, and was subject unto them. He went their messages, did their work, humbled Himself, as if this episode at Jerusalem had never been. Between His mother and Himself there was the true love that is built upon reverence. She reverenced Him. "She kept all those things, and pondered them in her heart." She knew the awful secret of His birth; and although the thought of His greatness had been somewhat obscured by her long ministrations to the weakness and helplessness of His

---

[1] That this is the true rendering, is forcibly argued by Dr. Field in a note in Farrar's *Gospel of St. Luke*, p. 368.

childhood, it could not be forgotten again; it had been brought to mind too sharply for that. After this crisis in His history He went home, and lived in peaceful solitude in the silence of the retired village,

"Voyaging through strange seas of thought alone."

The great use of this incident is to teach that Jesus Christ from His earliest years was conscious of His purpose. Without such a record as this we might have fancied that the consciousness of His life-work began with its execution. We are taught that it was not so, and that the years of silence were spent in consciousness of those powers which were to be exercised in the brief, intense years of His public ministry. He was developed by the influences of home, of nature, of the holy Scriptures, and, above all, by the Spirit of His Father working in Him.

III

THE SILENT YEARS OF JESUS,

AND

THE SILENT BUILDING OF THE TEMPLE

"There was neither hammer nor axe nor any tool of iron heard in the house, while it was in building."

"There is a day in spring,
When under all the earth the secret germs
Begin to stir and glow before they bud;
The wealth and festal pomps of midsummer
Lie in the heart of that inglorious day,
Which no man names with blessing, though its work
Is blest by all the world."

M. S.

CHAPTER III

THE SILENT YEARS OF JESUS, AND THE SILENT BUILDING OF THE TEMPLE

THERE are no fewer than eighteen years of the life of Christ of which we have no record, except what is contained in the words, "Is not this the carpenter?" It was said in His public life, "Never man spake like this man"; but we, with the Temple story fresh in our memory, may well say, "Never man kept silence like this man." We know what He could do, and how He could teach, and yet the whole history of His doings and teachings for these long years is summed up in the one word "carpenter." This strange silence reminds us of another strange silence. When the Temple of Solomon was being built, it grew silently: from the hands of the workmen who were gathered together, not a sound was heard. The Temple rose

"As Ilion like a mist rose into towers."

Jesus Christ likened Himself to the Temple. He spake of the Temple being destroyed and raised in three days, meaning thereby the temple of His body that was to fall in death, but to be built again fairer in the resurrection. And it is written in ancient prophecy, that He should sit a priest upon His throne, and build a temple to the Lord. So perhaps we may connect the two silences,—the silent growing of Solomon's Temple, and the silent years of Jesus. Perhaps the old builders, who had so much reverence in them, if we may judge from their work, thought that the noise and hammering, that might be fit enough for ordinary work, did not beseem the building of a holy temple to the Lord, which should grow, like the works of God's own building, in solemn silence. The great thought then before us is that Jesus grew in silence. Not merely the eighteen years, but we may say the whole thirty years, was a time of profound, hardly-broken silence. God's house was being built there, down at Nazareth, in the stillness.

We may consider the silence in three aspects. It was a time of restraint, a time of growth, and a time of preparation.

1. It was a time of restraint. We might have said suffering, for in one sense the word would be true, but the other word perhaps expresses the truth more nearly, —a time of self-denial, a time of obedience, manifesting itself in various ways. And, first of all, it manifested itself in the poverty of Jesus. Joseph was a carpenter in a provincial village, and Jesus shared his lot in life. They did not live in abject poverty; still they were poor, with nothing to spare for luxuries and superfluities, and nothing, probably, to store up for the future. Jesus in His after life looked a sterner poverty in the face, but He was poor now. There is a peculiar fitness about this. Jesus Christ came to save the world, and, under any conceivable condition of things,

poverty must be the lot of the great majority of human beings. It is so now; it probably must be so for ever. In Israel, the poor had a recognised standing in the national system. They were never to cease out of the land. "The poor ye have with you always." It is not needful that men should be abjectly, miserably poor. Most, if they will, may escape from that, but the rich must always be few; and so for the great mass, it is much to be able to go back to the home at Nazareth, and to remember that Christ and His relations were poor people, with the associations, the habits, the feelings, and the sympathies of the poor. He learned from actual experience what the limited dull life, lived day after day with little change until the last change of death, means, and by this He was prepared for the great work which He came to do. The motto of His ministry, read in the synagogue at Nazareth, was: "The Spirit of the Lord is upon me, because He hath anointed me to preach the gospel to the poor." When He went into the synagogue, He had the roll of Isaiah delivered to Him, and, disregarding the lesson for the day, as He had a right to do, He unwound the roll from the cylinder until this passage appeared. He read it, and then declared that that day the scripture had been fulfilled in their ears. The Galilean peasants who formed the listeners were of that class, and His words were for them. Poor men were His first disciples, and the grace of His example is specially seen in this, that "though He was rich, yet for our sakes He became poor, that we through His poverty might become rich." Those years at Nazareth would teach Him the needs of the poor. He would learn their sore struggles, their many temptations. He would know how hard it is for those whose strength is spent in the endeavour to gain bread, to think much of things unseen. He would perceive also how almost inevitably self-respect tends to disappear under the hard, brutalising conditions in which many led their life. Nazareth, small though it was, seems to have been notoriously wicked, and from the very beginning He would have opportunities of observing closely the misery, the ruin, and the shame of sin. He would learn also the proclamation of religion which poor people need,—as a religion which must satisfy the heart, and not make too great a demand on the understanding. The poor need religion, not as a material for speculative enterprise, but as a friend which can help them along the road of life and through the great change beyond it.[1] "For them life is always real,—its hopes, its misgivings, its joys, its heartaches, its catastrophes, its dim sense of the seriousness of being where and what we are, and of the possibilities before us, are quickened by poverty. The poor man, if religious at all, must believe in One who is no less an object of affection and obedience than the most awful and sublime of intellectual truths." He learned the lesson well, for the common people heard Him gladly. The poor had the gospel preached unto them, and received it. The Church of the apostles was the Church of the poor. It was, as has been said, the reproach and the glory of apostolic Christendom, that it first won its victories and then lavished its blessings chiefly among the poor. To win the poor, Jesus spoke in parables and in simple sayings, and with

[1] See Lidden, *University Sermons*, ii. 283.

deep sympathy; and if there is in the Christian Church now a want of feeling for the poor in their depressed multitudinousness,—in the great mass where the individual seems lost,—there has been a departure from the example and spirit of Christ.

Again, He was a labouring man, working, as the majority must always do, with His hands. It is quite impossible to evade the conclusion that He was a carpenter; and it is very probable that He must by His labour have earned the living of the humble household. Joseph seems to have died early; and Christ, as the oldest in the household,[1] would take upon Himself the burden of their maintenance. So He toiled there patiently at the carpenter's bench for many years. Why He chose His particular trade we cannot explain, further than to say that it was natural for Him to follow the occupation of Joseph. Allegorisers have suggested that in that labour He had continual occasion to ply the rule to judge what was right and straight, and that He was thus prepared for laying judgment to the line, and righteousness to the plummet. But the suggestion seems far-fetched. More important it is to note that He glorified common toil, and that He made mean the contempt in which the idle and those who work with the brain are too prone to regard those who labour with their hands.

Once more, He was obscure. The more fame is the object of ambition, the greater must be the number of those who are excluded from it. From its very nature, eminence can belong to but few, and the rest must live

[1] Not necessarily the oldest, but there is a considerable probability. See Plumptre, *Epistle of St. James*, p. 14 and foll.

simple, hidden, and unnoticed lives. He was content to live in that way, and so gives comfort to those who have no conspicuous position, who reached their place early, and who will never rise above it, and whose names will never travel beyond the very limited sphere of their home and work. He taught us that a great and noble life may be lived in obscurity, unnoticed and unpraised in the busy world. There is a lesson for those who seek to do great things and who despise little things. To do little things well may be to do great things. At least many who can do the great fail in the little. Peter said he could die for the Lord, but he could not keep awake for Him in the garden. Quiet things are those that in the long run win, and the quiet things done in obscurity and poverty may be ennobled and consecrated by the example of Jesus Christ. There are some who are so impatient of their obscurity, that if they cannot have fame they will have notoriety. But how different He was! How He restrained Himself! He saw everything going wrong. Amidst the scene of evil He would see passions running wild, and men's lives wrecked by their sin. He would hear God's word and God's mind misinterpreted, yet He kept silent till God's time came. He waited for the call; and though He grew in favour with men, and wound Himself in a strange fashion round their hearts, it is a singular thing that He was not marked as different from others. His brethren did not believe in Him. He was not even known as the strange son of the carpenter. He lived as others did; and when He came forward to do His work, those who had been all His life familiar with Him wondered as much as the strangers. They said,

"Is not this the carpenter?" We must remember that in these things He is more immediately our example than He is in the rest of His life. We cannot do the work of His public ministry,—we cannot speak His words, do His miracles, or endure His sufferings; but we are called upon to follow Him in quiet, toiling, humble, unconspicuous lives. So we miss much, if, in the thought of the public life of Christ, we forget the private life, which is a lesson for us even more, because it comes nearer us.

2. This period was a time of growth. As has been said, there are no materials in Scripture for very definite propositions as to the development of Christ. We know that there was an element which could not change, and another that was mutable. The growth was not an apparent development, but a real development. The point we specially note, however, is that He grew in silence. There is noise in building, but silence in growth. He grew as the flower grows, that turns its face to the sun, and travels all the arc after the light, and lets the rays pour into it till its broad disc grows broader and broader. He drank in the sunlight of God's presence—of His countenance. Ears of fairy fineness have been fabled to hear the flowers growing at midnight, but this is but fable, for we never heard growth. The great works of God grow in silence. Jesus grew as the old Temple grew, in silence of fitted stones. As the new building fitly framed together groweth unto a holy temple in the Lord, so He grew in silence. We may learn that if we are to grow in grace we must be silent. If the

Church is to grow, it must be without boasting and contention, by drinking in quietly the light of the face of God. In the glaring publicity given to the affairs of churches—the parades of statistics and the clatter of machinery—there cannot be much true growth. When we hear loud noise and ostentatious boasting, we may remember that the kingdom of God cometh not with observation, and that for the most part true progress does not come in that way. Hankerings after great demonstrations, to which the world will turn its eyes, show a misapprehension of true life; and what is true about the Church is true about the individual. Not in publicity, but in retirement and silence—in desert places—the spirit and teaching of Christ must be drunk in, if there is to rise a spiritual building of a holy life hid with Christ in God. Jesus Christ grew strong amidst that silence; and if we feel that we are not growing, let us ask ourselves whether we need rest and quiet, and whether waiting upon God would not renew the weakened and ebbing life.

3. This time was a time of preparation. The body and the mind were being prepared. Consider how the body must have been strengthened for the work He had to do under the sweet influences of nature, and the pure and healthy life that He lived. He was being fitted for the awful strain of His three years' ministry. When we remember how He toiled, we see that only a pure and uncontaminated body could have borne the weight of the effort. In these thirty years at Nazareth He was made strong for all that He had to do and endure. "Virtue," He said, when the woman touched

Him, "hath gone out of me." For three years strength was continually going out of Him; but for this expenditure He was prepared by the long season of repose. Not only was His body prepared, but His soul also. He learned the word of God so thoroughly that it became part of Himself. He learned the ways of men, for He must have been observant at all times. He increased in wisdom and in favour with God and man. At last, when the long time of preparation was over, the summons found Him ready, and His readiness is proved by the whole record of His ministry. "What a long foreground you must have had for such a start!" said one writer to another who had published his first book late in life. So there was a long foreground, but it was a foreground for the three years' ministry.

These eighteen years of silence must have been lived, for they could not have been imagined. Exactly the reverse would have been the product of human imagination. He who had so wondrously impressed the teachers at Jerusalem, would remain there, and take, sooner than any had ever done, the highest place amongst the sages. He would work wonders, and His life would be filled with memorable deeds and words. That is how we should have imagined it, but God's plan was that He should wait eighteen years in a wise passiveness.

It was a time of preparation, and we are able to trace what He prepared for; but if we do not, we need not suppose that the time was lost. Many seem, so far as we can see, to prepare all their lives for the uttering of one sentence—the doing of one deed; and others—a far more numerous class—seem to prepare all their lives for a work that never comes. Through slow, dull years they toil on, and die without having an opportunity for doing any great deed, or speaking any life-giving word. Has the time of preparation been lost? No, because there is an eternity beyond. Had Moses died away in Midian, would his life have been thrown away? No, for there is an eternity to work in. Many will die, and their life will have been a time of preparation for higher service which never came, and we are inclined to say life is lost. But so long as there is a whole eternity in which to develop the preparation of time, that should never be said. A deep lesson for life to most of us is, that the great achievements are to be done not on this side, but on the other side of death. Nowhere does faith show itself more clear and victorious, than in one who goes on to the very end laboriously cultivating every power, although no outlet for exercise is visible. To be irritably and fretfully anxious for a field in which to display one's talent, is to fail in trust. The calm, unsolicitous endeavour after the perfection of our nature, and the committal to God of the instrument when it has been tempered, to use where and when He pleases, is a noble achievement of faith. And so, if we are relegated to obscurity, or compelled to be passive when we are willing to be active, and when we think our instruments are ready, let us spend the time not in fretting but in preparing,—in strengthening our wills, kindling our inspirations, cultivating our faculties,—and then, when the word falls upon our listening ears, we shall be ready to say, "Here am I; Thou hast called me at last, and I am before Thee with all my powers and my opportunities." Jesus Christ spent eighteen years at Nazareth in silence. The result of them was,—"a few years of action, but of action concentrated, intense, infinite. Not one word, not one deed, which did not tell, and which will not tell, upon the universe for ever. Eighteen years of silence, and then the regeneration of the world accomplished, His Father's business done!"

IV
JOHN BAPTIST AND THE BAPTISM OF CHRIST

"Among them that are born of women there hath not risen a greater than John the Baptist: nevertheless he that is least in the kingdom of heaven is greater than he."

"He the last star of parting night,
And we the children of the dawn."

CHAPTER IV

JOHN BAPTIST AND THE BAPTISM OF CHRIST

WE are justly suspicious of summary judgments on so complex a thing as a man's life and work. Human life and character are so mixed and mysterious, that we do not care to have the secret of a man's history packed into a neat epigram. But of John the Baptist we have a brief judgment passed by the Master and the Judge of souls. "Among them that are born of women," said He, "there hath not risen a greater than John the Baptist: nevertheless he that is least in the kingdom of heaven is greater than he." Here we have an anticipation of the judgment-seat, and here we have also some justification of our suspicion of human judgments, for neither in one part of the judgment nor in the other do we find what we should have expected to find. There are men in history whom we should be inclined to place higher than John; and certainly we should shrink from saying that the least and humblest believer was greater than he. But the judgment of Christ is our unerring guide, and, after glancing at the history, we shall dwell upon what it tells us of the greatness and littleness of John the Baptist.

In the first period of John's life we find him in

the wilderness, weary of the hollowness and untruth of the world. He went into the desert to commune with his own soul. During that period his mind had intimate converse with the prophets of the old covenant. The marks of their influence and that of the desert scenery appear prominently in his after teaching. He was not alone in the desert in vain. Away from the deceit of man, he found truth at last. The whole truth was not disclosed to him, but a message was given which he might with certainty communicate to his generation. The message once gained, he could not waste it on the desert air. He had to pay the debt he owed to his kind. The word burned within him; he was weary of forbearing, and could not stay; and, without taking time to adapt his ways and speech to the polished uses of society, this strong son of the desert presented himself before the startled Jews, and proclaimed that he was the forerunner of the Messiah, and that the Messiah was near at hand—even at the door.

It is in accordance with the way of God to guide history by a gradual process,—to give men indications of His coming work and will. Streaks herald the dawn, and the dawn the day. The long line of prophets had foretold the coming of Jesus, but still the day lingered, and their voices had become silent. Time, however, had not ceased to flow, and time brought with it the coming of Christ. When He was near, John was appointed to give warning, and to tell them that the Saviour, whom they had long looked for, was at last nigh.

He had to tell them, further, that they were not

ready for His coming. Their life, unreal and sinful, must be thoroughly reformed before they could meet the King with welcome. The King was coming to lay His axe to the old Jewish tree. He came with His fan in His hand throughly to purge His floor, and to cast the chaff into the fire. "Repent!" was the message of this stern prophet,—a message not addressed to one, or to a class, but to all,—a message which urged a reform that went much deeper than the outside, and involved, indeed, an entire revolution of the inner nature: "Repent, for the kingdom of heaven is at hand."

Most men who can speak directly and sincerely to heart and conscience, find an unhoped-for readiness of response, and that often in the most unlikely quarters. To one like John, whose sincerity was so undeniable, who had won the truth he taught with such earnest struggle, a welcome was given so enthusiastic that it must have surprised himself. His uncompromising denunciations of sin did not awake hostility, but drew around him even the proud Scribes and Pharisees. He did not lower his message for his hearers, but urged upon those who thought they had touched perfection in their obedience to the law, their need to flee from the wrath to come. Hollow sick hearts found him, as they always find a man who is content to speak the true word of God; and how deep the heart-sickness was which then oppressed the nation, may be judged from the fact that the whole region went out to the desert to him, confessing their sins. Many would have been drawn by the news of the approaching footfalls of the Messiah, but besides that, there was the deep sense of sin and unworthiness which he had awakened in their spirits.

But though he could indicate the disease and make it felt, he could not cure it. He could only say, "Repent!" He baptized, indeed, but his baptism was with water. He could not reach down to the inmost defilement and take it away. The water was a fit emblem of the cold, unsatisfying, ineffectual character of his ministry, just as the fire with which Jesus Christ baptized was an emblem of the warming, searching character of His. After Jesus came, John proclaimed, "Behold the Lamb of God, that taketh away the sin of the world." That these words have a reference to the Old Testament idea of the suffering Servant of God, cannot reasonably be disputed.[1] After the intense agony of the wilderness, Christ's appearance, as well as the story of His self-abnegation, would bring to mind the afflicted Servant of the 53rd chapter of Isaiah. But the words were a special inspiration in special circumstances; and it is clear from the subsequent narrative that the two conceptions of Christ—as the sufferer and the judge—were never harmoniously adjusted in the Baptist's mind. This witness to the atoning Lamb he was not long allowed to bear. He was the herald of the dawn, but the new kingdom to which he pointed he did not enter, and he could not fully comprehend.

In the last period of John's life we find him in the court of Herod. Here he underwent the real trial of his life. In the air of the desert, amid the free winds of heaven, and beneath the open sky, he might well

---

[1] See Reynolds' *John the Baptist*, p. 376, and Westcott *in loc.*

bear an undaunted witness; but when his chainless spirit was taken into the enervating atmosphere of a court, his dangers greatly increased. Will he, we ask, turn out a mere court preacher, like those with whom history has made us only too familiar? Will he trim and abate his message to suit kingly ears? Will he wink hard at kingly vices? Nay, verily; to Herod he was like an incarnate conscience. The vicious, weak, dissolute king, not yet unvisited by better impulses and higher promptings, viewed him as a just man and a holy, and observed many of his injunctions. One darling vice, however, he could not surrender. He was living in an incestuous connection with his brother Philip's wife, and the voice of the stern preacher would not cease saying, "It is not lawful for thee to have her." Systematically to disobey conscience in one injunction, is to disobey in all, and the words, "It is not lawful for thee to have her," ringing constantly in the ears of Herod and his guilty paramour, made life unbearable. So he did what many a one has done before and since, he tried to muffle his conscience,— not, at first, to extinguish it entirely. He put John into a dungeon, where his protest could not be heard in the banqueting halls of the castle. Still, muffled though the voice was, it sometimes made its way into the ears of the guilty sinners. Just as conscience comes sometimes to an abandoned man in breaks and pauses of revelry, and speaks then more stingingly than it used to do when he talked with it hourly, so Herod would, in spite of himself, be drawn sometimes down the dismal stairs to where the prophet was lying, and come back with his heart pained and trembling, as never before,—come back with a gloom that reflected itself in his guilty consort, till at length she resolved that this voice should be silenced for ever. So in one night of mad revelry the king promised to give to a dancing girl whatever she asked, even to the half of his kingdom. At her mother's prompting she asked the prophet's head, and the king, though he was exceeding sorry,—for no man murders his conscience willingly, his conscience being part of himself, and the murder a suicide,—yet nevertheless he gave consent, and John was beheaded in the dungeon. The maiden brought her frightful gift under the glaring lights: Herod gazed on the accusing face, and knew that he had killed his conscience. Henceforth he was not troubled, except by spectral fears. He could meet Jesus without a blush, and ask Him about many things. But to Herod Jesus observed a boding fateful silence, for to those who have slain their conscience the lips of the Incarnate Word are for ever locked.

The greatness of John the Baptist is announced in striking and emphatic words by our Saviour. None of all that went before was greater than he. His greatness appears mainly in his courage. There is no virtue so popular as courage. No men win the heart of a nation as do its defenders by land and sea. Names like Wellington and Nelson stir the blood of the people as the names of statesmen and men of letters never can. This admiration is often misplaced. Courage—mere courage—is frequently nothing more than brute insensibility to danger,—an insensibility which refined natures often do not possess. Still, overrated as the virtue may be, the popular instinct is not wrong, for true courage reposes upon very deep qualities. John's courage appeared in his championship of truth. He did not palter with the truth to gain the hearts of men. He did not shrink from telling the most self-righteous of his hearers that they were a generation of vipers. To king and to Pharisee alike he called "Repent!" and to both he asserted the sovereignty of God's immutable law. He was true in pointing on to Christ. He himself was not the Christ, but a voice that announced His coming. Men were not to look upon him and see in him a pretender to faultless virtue. They were to give heed to the message, looking away from the imperfect messenger, who was not worthy to unloose the shoe latchet of the Perfect One who was coming. In spite of all temptation to arrogate to himself more than was rightfully his due, John continued to deny that he was the Christ, and to affirm that he was not fit to be compared with the Christ.

This courage reposed, first of all, upon faith. The Lord Jesus, summing up his life, emphasised this. "John," He said, "was not a reed shaken by the wind,"—the stormy wind of popular fury, or the milder but not less dangerous breezes of popular applause. His belief was not a hearsay creed: his soul built upon real truths. He knew that Christ was before him, and that Christ was to come as the perfect and accredited Messenger of God. He knew that all men before Christ were guilty, and that all needed to repent. From these faiths nothing could move him away.

Again, his courage reposed on independence. To be

dependent on the world is to be afraid of the world; but he was content to live on what the desert could afford him. From man he needed nothing, and sought nothing. He was, our Lord says, not luxurious,—not a wearer of soft clothing,—but a hardy child of nature. He owed the world nothing but the truth, and fully and boldly did he pay that debt.

And yet more, he was disinterested. He might have reaped earthly fruits of his work, but he did not seek to do so. He might have founded a school, and his disciples were disappointed that he did not. He might have asserted with a partial and temporary measure of success his claims against the rising ascendancy of Christ, but his words were, "He must increase, but I must decrease." He was a prophet, and more than a prophet, for he was a baptizer. Still he knew that his preaching and baptism were unsatisfying and incomplete, and he pointed on to One who could baptize with the Holy Ghost and with fire. This deep, well-grounded, dauntless courage and disinterestedness won the warm admiration of Christ, who declared that of all the great servants of God that had gone before, none was greater than this prisoner of Herod.

If we were puzzled by the first part of the judgment, much more are we perplexed by the second: "He that is least in the kingdom of heaven is greater than he." "What!" we say; "is it possible that the weakest Christian in the Church—and how weak such an one may be each may know—is greater than John the Baptist?" "Yes," we must reply, for this is not a question of nature, but one of grace. The life of the new kingdom is such that it infinitely ennobles the receiver. John was the last star of the departing night. We are the children of the dawn, and the dawn has made us greater than he. He could point men on, but he could not enable them to attain. His system was terror, but terror is transitory while the evil day lingers. He was always outside of the kingdom, rejoicing in its coming, but never entering in.

He wanted the life of the new kingdom. His life is a very sunless one. There are few lives that inspire a deeper compassion. He was, like Moses, led to the threshold, and died there. At the last he sent the question to Christ: "Art thou He that should come, or do we look for another?" The question was more than the mere result of despondency. It is true that the child of the desert was confined, and that a morbid weariness may have had much to do with it. But Christ's grave reply shows that there was something more. There was a radical misconception of the nature of Christ's kingdom. The kingdom, as preached by Christ, was good news; as preached by John, it was awful news. John spoke of a Judge coming to discriminate and punish; Jesus, of a Father who was ready to receive and pardon the guiltiest. John missed in Christ the axe and the fan of which he had spoken. He looked for Christ to do the work of avenging and judging; and lo! no weapons were seen in His hands, and His voice was not one of terror. Therefore it was that John asked whether He was the Messiah; and therefore it was that Christ recited His gentle works, and declared of John that the least in the kingdom was greater than he.

The life of the kingdom, as we have said, ennobles the least member of it. A statue may be polished with consummate skill, till the marble seems nigh to breathing; but the most shapeless product in the kingdom of life is greater than the greatest achievement of the sculptor. So the least Christian who has received the life of the kingdom of heaven is greater than John.

Besides, he wanted the power of the new kingdom. He did no miracles,—he did no outward miracle, and no inward miracle. He could not change the heart, or baptize with the Spirit. Greater things than outward miracles could the disciples in the kingdom of heaven do through the power that rested on them, but that power did not come to him.

If John cannot be compared with the least in the kingdom of heaven, much less can he be compared with the Master of that kingdom. The two come together in a very striking way. What their relations were in early years we cannot tell. It is probable that John knew Jesus, though he may not have met Him for many years. John was baptizing by the river, and when Jesus approached him a voice within whispered who this peasant was, and he saw in an instant how wide was the gulf between Him and the others who came to be baptized,—nay, between Him and the baptizer. But Jesus made His purpose known, and said He would be baptized, because it became Him to fulfil all righteousness. He did not disclaim the homage that John paid Him,—He never disclaimed homage, however great,—but He declared that the head and representative of the people should prepare their way. He was to die for them, and to bear the weight of their sins, and He would identify Himself with them in their most humbling experiences. So He went down into the water,—not, indeed, to be cleansed by it,—rather, as an old writer says, to cleanse it;[1] and the divine voice declared: "This is my beloved Son, in whom I am well pleased." He descended into the water, just as He submitted in His early years to the Jewish law. His being baptized was part of His unutterable humiliation. Jesus pledged Himself to the fulfilment of all righteousness on behalf of the race whom He had come to save, and the divine Spirit was given to Him to prepare Him for the rest of the work. He had the Spirit before. Here it was given to Him with a new richness to equip Him for the new functions He was now to perform, and in His strength He went forward.

It might be pointed out that Christ is complete, while John was incomplete. Christ was the centre of truth, yea, the truth beyond which we cannot advance. John was but the vestibule into the temple. John was conscious of imperfection, and pointed from the messenger who was human, to the message that was divine. Jesus came not merely to preach the gospel, but to be the gospel, and challenged the strictest scrutiny, both of Himself and of His message. John, for all his unfaltering boldness, erred and doubted. Christ made no mistake—no retractation. John died as a victim—the victim of a lustful woman. Jesus died as a priest; no man took His life from Him. John's death did nothing for the race; Christ's death saved the race. There was no story of the resurrection of

[1] See Keim, ii. 274-276, and Note B.

John. His grave was the end of his school. When the disciples laid in the tomb his awful and headless dust, they gradually disorganised. Jesus died and rose again, and by His resurrection drew His disciples together. All are unsatisfying and incomplete save Christ. We ascend till we come to Him; further we cannot go.

Such a life and death as John's cannot be explained, without the faith of immortality. His life, viewed from an earthly standpoint, was a complete and dreary failure. But his death was an escape from the twofold prison—the prison of Herod and the prison of his own doubts—into wide and utter liberty. It was an entrance into the kingdom of heaven, where that kingdom is realised in its purity and completeness.

V
THE TEMPTATION OF CHRIST

"To him that overcometh will I grant to sit with me in my throne, even as I also overcame, and am set down with my Father in His throne."

"The day when he, Pride's lord and man's,
Showed all earth's kingdoms at a glance
To Him before whose countenance
The years recede, the years advance."

ROSSETTI.

CHAPTER V

THE TEMPTATION OF CHRIST

THE temptation of Christ followed His baptism, and must be viewed in connection with it. When God gives armour, He soon puts it to the proof, and so the strength given at the baptism was soon tested in the wilderness. The first Adam fell from the garden to the wilderness, and so in the wilderness the second Adam takes up and wins the battle. He was led by the Spirit into the wilderness—led by the good Spirit to be tempted of the evil. "The Spirit," says Mark, "driveth Him into the wilderness,"—an expression we may fairly take as showing how great is the pain of temptation, and how Christ shrank from it. Temptation is not to be avoided by flying into solitude, for there the Lord met with the evil spirit.

Into some difficulties connected with this subject we do not intend to enter, simply because it does not appear that there are materials for the solution of these problems. That there is a personal devil, and that he was the agent in the temptation, we assume as the plain teaching of Scripture, confirmed by many mysterious passages of life. It has been well said that though the devil may be expelled from theology, he cannot be got out of the world, so marred by traces of his work. We do not attempt to explain how the sinless Christ could be tempted. We assume that a sinless manhood can be tempted, and further, that to a sinless nature temptation must come from the outside, and not from within; and thus we find it here.

1. The first temptation, "If thou be the Son of God, command that these stones be made bread," was addressed to Jesus after forty days of fasting. During these days He had been sustained, not by the power of His divine nature, but by the great rapture of spiritual gladness which upbore Him. When these had passed, He was torn by the pangs of hunger, and here the temptation of Satan comes in.

"If thou be the Son of God." After the manner of the tempter, he makes the truth problematical. He disparages the Sonship of the Saviour. As in Paradise he had said, "Yea, hath God said," so now to the hungry, weary Christ he says, "If thou be the Son of God, command that these stones be made bread." The stones to the sick eyes of a hungry man had the shape of loaves, and one word from Him would have turned them to food. Why was the word not spoken? Because, if He had spoken it, He would have undone His incarnation, by drawing back from the lot of the race with which He had identified Himself. He would also have shown a want of trust in the divine providence, that was able to feed Him without His using any miraculous energy. "Man shall not live by bread alone, but by everything that proceedeth out of the mouth of God." He did not care to assert His Godship then. "*Man*," He says, "shall not live by bread alone."

Bread can feed man, because God made it so; but if God pleased, He might make the bare wind of the desert a banquet. Jesus has meat to eat that the tempter knows not of.

We may view these separate temptations, first, as illustrating the identity of Christ with His brethren; and, secondly, as showing the nature of the temptations wherewith He was assailed all His life. Leaving the second use to be considered afterwards, let us see how this first temptation is presented to us by the tempter in our own lives. To make bread may be called the life-work of most, and in the effort we are assailed continually by satanic suggestions. Thus, if I give up my convictions, it will open the way to a lucrative position. Tricks of trade would help me; my rivals use them, and if I do not I must perish. I must live. The answer is, There is no need that a man should live, but there is need that he should be righteous. He will not die if he trusts in God. Man lives by everything that proceedeth from God's mouth. The old answer of Jesus Christ is enough for us in the hour of temptation, which comes, we may say, to all. Again, man is sometimes destroyed by his very blessings. Bread is abundant, and he needs nothing more. That staff is broken; and instead of being destroyed he is saved, for it is then, and not till then, that he begins to live upon God. We may even extend this, and say that this temptation illustrates all those that come under the description of the apostle, "the lust of the flesh."

2. He was taken next to the holy city, as Matthew describes it, the city so dear to the Jews, and to the

most sacred place there,—to the Temple, and to the pinnacle of the Temple. It was a masterpiece of Satan to take Him there. If He had yielded there, it would have been a defeat indeed. We learn to take care of places that seem secure. This was the most unlikely place for temptation, and yet there the enemy was busy. With steady foot and wary eye, and the heart braced for conflict, do we need to tread even in those places where we expect Satan least.

He was tempted to presumption: "If thou be the Son of God, cast thyself down." The tempter, as if he had learned a lesson from Christ's quotation of Scripture, quotes Scripture himself. "Cast thyself down," he says, "and thou shalt drop into the soft arms of waiting angels who have charge to keep thee." He left out the words, "In all thy ways." The way downward from the Temple was not a way of God, and in that way there was no promise that He should be kept. Arguments from Scripture are the best or the worst of arguments; and how we should use Scripture, we are taught by Jesus when He says, "It is written—It is written again." By comparison and balancing we learn the truth. "Thou shalt not tempt the Lord thy God"; which means, Thou shalt not idly put God's friendship to the proof; thou shalt not rush needlessly into danger; thou shalt not rashly undertake great enterprises before thou art sent. "Cast thyself down!" There is no sin that is not voluntary. The tempter could bring Christ to the pinnacle of the Temple, but he could not cast Him down. Jesus would not tempt the Lord His God. He withstood in the evil day, and having done all, He stood. This temptation is illustrated in our experience by our frequent incitements to presumption, to foolish hazarding, and to needless testing of God's promises. When it was proposed some years ago to test the reality of God's answer to prayer in the healing of the sick, the Lord our God was tempted. Men apparently find it difficult to see the sin as it applies to God. They can understand it very well in the lower planes of human life. When one friend puts the friendship of another to needless and cruel tests and strains, such conduct is justly resented. And why? Because it shows a want of faith in the friendship. A friendship really trusted would not be so tried. All these experiments on God, these rash misreadings of His promises, spring at bottom from a want of faith. Calm trust in God does not need nervously to prove Him; it rests in settled peace.

3. The last temptation was the worst of all. The two stood together on a lofty peak, with all the kingdoms of the world and the glory of them spread beneath them. Satan, arrayed, we may conjecture, like an angel of light, stood in his majesty beside the worn and weary Christ, and pointed to the glittering glories around,—all the kingdoms of the world and the glory of them; and all were to be His if He would kneel for a moment and worship,—one touch of the knees upon the snow, and the power would be His own. We do not understand this temptation if we suppose that Christ was attracted by the outward glitter and show. He saw from the mountain the misery of the world,—hearts beating under the sway of the evil prince, to whom the world had been

delivered. God's love was abused or unknown, God's best gifts were working evil. And Satan said, "This is in my power, for these things are delivered unto me." He does not dare to say more than the truth. He was not prince of the world by victory—only by sufferance. This influence he held by the tenure of God's will. And now he says to Christ, "If thou wilt worship me, thou shalt have the rule. Thou shalt stanch all wounds, dry all tears, heal all suffering, repair what I have done so much to waste and ruin; and more, thou shalt have all this sway in a moment." Christ sought this dominion. He was to die to gain this dominion; but instead of the sorrowful way of the cross, a new road that would bring Him instantly to the end is pointed out. This was the strongest and the most wicked of the temptations, and was repelled with awful violence: "Get thee behind me, Satan." There is no argument here; the moment was too terrible a one for fencing. The attack is made and repelled, and the temptation is over.

For Christ the way to kinghood lay through a deep valley. The shortest way to the kingdom is not the best. Through much tribulation we must enter the kingdom of God.

The lesson for us is, that influence for good may be bought too dear. To desire to have more power to wield for God in this world—nay, to reach out with longing to the time when we shall sit on the right hand of the Son of God—is not base but noble. Only to these great things we must ascend by God's own ladder, and to climb any other way is to change the lofty ambition to a vile appetite. The happiness of any heaven must, it has been well said, consist in certain inner voices. Wherever conscience is compromised with for any gain whatever, the gain turns out worthless. An eternity of usefulness bought by one moment of sin is bought too dear. Many acquire wealth unlawfully, and seek to wipe away the sin by a noble beneficence. Others gain reputation by dishonest means, and try to quiet their consciences by using the influence for Christ. But it is in vain. They have fallen down to Satan to gain the kingdom, and so the kingdom is valueless. The temptation is a very subtle one, and it must be repelled with absolute and instant rejection, as we see that Christ repelled it.

The devil leaveth Him *for a season*. His fiery darts were all quenched and blunted, and the adversary fled. What is the force of these words,—for a season? Some consider that they signify the assault at the close of His ministry, when He was tempted in the garden. But it is far more in accordance with the facts of His life to read the words as referring to the continual battle of His life. He Himself, as we have often occasion to remark, lets a deep silence brood for the most part over His own inward experience; and thus it was necessary, perhaps, that we should have two such distinct and strongly-marked scenes of temptation as the conflicts in the wilderness and in Gethsemane. But in one of the deeply instructive revealings of His inner life, He says to His disciples, "Ye are they who have continued with me in my temptations." "My temptations": that is the description of His life. There was not a temptation at the beginning and at the end, and a clear space between, but the battle was fought all through His life. And if there be proof, or rather record, awanting of it, that does not make it less terrible, for mortal struggles are waged often in grim silence. His last word, "I have overcome the world," tells how sharp the strife had been, which is remembered even in heaven, as He speaks to His militant Church, and tells them that they shall overcome "even as I also overcame." "As on some battlefield, whence all traces of the agony and fury have passed away, the harvests wave and larks sing where blood ran and men groaned their lives out, some gravestone raised by the victors remains, and only the trophy tells of the forgotten fight, so the monumental word, 'I have overcome,' stands to all ages as the record of the silent, lifelong conflict."

We may trace, although imperfectly, how the devil returned and plied Him with the same temptations all His life through.

1. He was tempted all His life by bodily pain and privation. Imaginative reverence tends to soften the sharp angles of truth, and makes us forget that Jesus Christ was poor. He had nothing that He could call His own, and when He died He left nothing behind Him but His seamless robe. He had said, "Lay not up for yourselves treasures on earth," and He had obeyed His own precepts. There was no secret hoard hidden from the keen eye of Judas the treasurer. He was hungry, and sought to feed Himself from a fig-tree by the way. He was tired, and He slept in

The Temptation of Christ

the fishing-boat. He had nothing to pay His tribute with. And when He was to reply to the captious question of the Pharisee, He said, " Bring me a penny." He had nowhere to lay His head in life or in death. It was a borrowed grave in which He took His short sleep. He was therefore plied incessantly with the temptation to make Himself rich amidst all those treasures which a word from His lips could have unlocked. But He never did so. In His poverty He did not cease to be God. The very examples of His poverty which we have quoted, have definite and strange marks of His divinity. He stilled the storm from the boat where He had been sleeping, with the wooden pillow beneath His head. He burst the bonds of death, and came out of the borrowed grave a conqueror over the last enemy. But provide for Himself He did not, and He would not. As a commander in a famine-stricken city refuses exemption from the lot of his fellow-soldiers, so our Leader and Commander refuses to listen to the solicitudes of His need, and lived and died poor. A great thinker, we are told,[1] was especially pitiful to those who sinned from the pangs of poverty and hunger. Such sin might be excused if any sin could be. We could understand that, and the more easily in the case of one who had once been rich. He was rich once—with an amplitude of wealth we cannot comprehend. He needed not ever to have been poor. Stones would have turned into bread at a word from Him. But for our sakes He became poor, and remained poor, that we through His poverty might become rich.

[1] Foster.

2. Again, there was a temptation to use His supernatural power. He had taken the resolution neither to court danger in reliance upon superhuman power, nor needlessly to free Himself from it. And we find instances of this in the sequel. For example, when His enemies sought to kill Him, He quietly departed. He did not suffer them to touch Him. And how merciful was this, for, had they touched Him before the time, they would have fallen dead as they did who profanely handled the ark of God. No one could take His life from Him; but when His time came, He surrendered Himself to the human wills that so blindly destroyed Him. But until then He was safe; yet not safe by undue use of His divine power. When Peter took Him aside, and said, "Be it far from thee, Lord: this shall not be unto thee," He replied, "Get thee behind me, Satan," treating the words of the apostle as another suggestion of the baffled spirit.

3. Again, He rejected a false Messiahship, accordant with the worldly spirit of Judaism, in favour of an inward kingdom to be developed by the power of the divine Spirit. All the kingdoms of the world, and all the glory of them, were to be His at last, but He would not grasp His sceptre too soon. When they sought to make Him a king by force, He left them and went into solitude. It was better to be alone than to be the creature of such creatures. He would not please His disciples by taking a temporal kingship, which they should share in Jerusalem. He becomes King by dying. His cross is His throne. His cross was at once the intense superlative of all temptations and the final answer to the tempter. When He died, His feet

The Temptation of Christ

like fine brass bruised the head of the great enemy of mankind.

In conclusion, we do not forget that He had to wrestle with the Evil One at the end. The struggle was one of peculiar intensity. He was tried by pain, as He had been aforetime by pleasure. His consistency was tested by agony of body and mind. But as He had overcome the tempter at the first, so He overcame him at the last. Still this does not lead us to forget that He Himself described the space between the wilderness temptation and the temptation at the end as "my temptations." Not "my sorrows," "my difficulties," "my pains," but "my temptations." His virtue was not cloistered and untried. It was subjected to the hottest fire of the struggle, and came out unscathed. He was victorious in the end; and yet how significant it is, that when He describes His life, it should come before Him as "my temptations"![1]

[1] See Note C.

VI
THE OBJECT AND CLAIMS OF CHRIST

"This is a faithful saying, and worthy of all acceptation, that Christ Jesus came into the world to save sinners."

"He did not come to judge the world, He did not come to blame;
He did not only come to seek,—it was to save He came:
And when we call Him Saviour, then we call Him by His name."

DORA GREENWELL.

CHAPTER VI

THE OBJECT AND CLAIMS OF CHRIST

THE object of Christ was defined in different ways by Himself, but ultimately is perhaps most fully expressed in the saying: "The Son of man is come to seek and to save that which was lost." In the apostolic Church the saying was current in this form: "Christ Jesus came into the world to save sinners." Who first expressed it so we cannot tell. Like many of the most beautiful things and thoughts, it is the work of an unknown soul. It immediately found welcome, and was passed from mouth to mouth, and lodged in memory after memory. At last the apostle took it up and indorsed it with his authority, declaring it to be a faithful saying, and worthy of all acceptation. We take it as an infallible guide in teaching us the purpose of the eternal God, entering into time and submitting to the bonds of flesh.

The description of man, as lost, claims our attention first. Lost means lost to God. God had lost man, and He was grieved by the loss,—how deeply grieved we should not have dared to imagine, had not the Saviour Himself explained it in three of His most touching parables. Man was missed by God as a shepherd misses one sheep out of a hundred—as a woman misses one silver piece out of a little hoard of ten;[1] or, to put it more adequately, as a father misses his younger son in a house where there are but two. Man's fall is God's loss. In another aspect man's fall is man's sin. The sin of man in wandering from God is depicted in the very darkest hues. It is a mark of a revelation from God that it does not extenuate the guilt of sin, or minimise the awfulness of its consequences. He who came to save sinners was He who spake the most terrible things of sin. Further, this wandering from God not only involved God in loss, but also the soul in loss. To be absent from God was to be dead. That was not life which was lived away from righteousness, truth, purity, and all high influences that flow from heaven. Such a life might be quick and energetic so far as earthly interests and aims were concerned, but this very activity only served to throw into darker relief its deadness to all great ends and issues. Man had sinned, man was lost, man was dead in trespasses and sins.

But, strict as His judgment of sin was, and fiery His indignation against it, He did not give a despairing view of it. He taught that deep as were the misery and ruin into which man was plunged by sin, he might nevertheless be saved from them,—yea, brought to the very height of purity and perfection. He might win all that he had ever lost, and more. There is nothing more striking than the way in which the Bible describes the disease and shame of sin, and then calmly fronts

---

[1] The small intrinsic value makes the emblems a better type of the despised publicans and sinners.

the question how a being so marred and degraded can be restored. Further, He taught that it was worth while to save man whatever the expenditure might be; for man, however far he had wandered, had still the image of God. As one may read the sacred writing of an old manuscript beneath all the disfiguring inscriptions of later days, so Jesus saw in the soul of the meanest Syrian slave, through all erasures and blots, the stamp of God. He never shared in the view, to which there is so much to incline us, that man is too sinful and too insignificant to be worth the pains and the effort of God. The lost thing was precious enough to bring Him down from heaven that He might save it. He came to seek and to save that which was lost. He came into the world that the world through Him might be saved. Accordingly He gave no place to the distinctions of race. As He Himself stood above the national and secular peculiarities of His place and time, as He was a foreigner in no land, but a citizen of every tongue and kindred,—the Son of man,—His heart was not bounded by any of the separating walls which confine us. Rank and wealth were nothing to Him. Before His eyes nothing was common and unclean. He came not to save a particular race, but a world. So large a thought conceived and expressed at a time when great ideas were unfamiliar, and little provinces of human love and trust were rigorously mapped out,—such a thought was divine. The father seeks the salvation of the family, the citizen of the city, the patriot of the country; but the Son of man came to seek and to save the whole world. This largeness of sympathy was fully consistent with the most loving individual regard. He did not love the world without caring for the individuals of the world. He loved man because He loved men. He had special friendships. He associated Himself with special members of guilty and degraded classes. His love was the aggregate of personal attachments, and each object of His love is regarded with a solitary affection as true and as heedful as though there were none other in all the world to share it.

When He addressed Himself to the salvation of the lost, He did not do so by ignoring the great problem which had to be solved. He did not content Himself with improving the condition of society. Nothing has done so much to raise society as the work of Christ. But that taken alone was not His object. He did not lower the standard of divine holiness; indeed, He elevated it far higher than ever it had been raised; and yet He did not repel men by its exhibition, but so showed it as to make men enamoured of goodness. He did not address Himself to the cultivation of mind, for the highest enlightenment may be present along with entire spiritual ruin. Nor was he content even with improved conduct and better feeling. Nothing would satisfy Him short of the weakening and the ultimate expulsion of the power of sin. The plague of the heart, the one real evil and deep disease of humanity, the rebellion against our Lord and God,— these He dealt with; and the expulsion of them, and the subjugation of the will to Himself, was the aim short of which He could not be satisfied. The bound will had to be liberated from its chains, and made to obey Him who was its rightful King. This great surrender was faith in Himself. The soul that once trusted Him was back in the old true way. It had ceased from straying, and was returned to the Shepherd and Bishop of souls.

Before this union could be accomplished,—before His purpose of mercy to the race could be realised,—He had to die. It is this which separates Christ so widely from every human teacher. Death comes to all men as the mark of weakness, failure, and guilt. But how could it come to Him who was the Son of God? Death comes to other workers to end their work, but to Him it came as His work. We shall miss entirely the whole meaning of the life and death of Christ, if we take His death as an incident which might have been averted, and which He hoped to avert. He came into the world to save sinners, and for their salvation it was needful that He should die. Men were to be saved by faith in Him, but the object of their faith was to be the Son of man lifted up. He was not torn in pieces, by venturing in a rash moment too near the whirling wheel of the world's evil. He saw the end before Him from the beginning, and might have shunned it had He so pleased; but to shun it would have been to leave to their doom sinful, straying men. This has always been an enigma to the world. When the Jews saw Him nailed to the cross and in the hold of death, they judged His claim to be practically settled. Even His own disciples, when they saw Him in the tomb, abandoned their hopes. "We trusted," said they, "that it had been He who should have redeemed Israel." He Himself shrank from death with all the natural shrinking of a pure and vigorous human nature; but He distinctly recognised that not to die was to be barren, —to abide alone,—and that death would be as the falling of a corn of wheat into the ground, which, dying, bringeth forth much fruit.

How His death was to be thus fruitful, we do not at present attempt to explain. The fact to be insisted on is, that He freely willed to die for us. His life was not taken from Him whether He would or not, but by the free will of His love and pity He gave Himself up that we might be redeemed.

Further, He declared Himself to be the only source of life. He did not stand side by side with other ministers and channels of grace. He did not allow His teaching to take a place as one form out of many, but declared that He had a monopoly of truth, that He had the secret of salvation, that there was salvation in none other; that though human modes might affect the fate of man in this world, nothing could really influence for good the hereafter, save faith in Him. The high charity that brought Him down to give light to them in the shadow of death, made Him declare that His light was the true light, and that all others would fail and go out; that to save man was to restore him to God in this life, and to begin that purification which would be completed in the other life when God would be seen face to face. To be lost to God was a state which grew steadily darker and more painful amongst the eternal issues beyond the grave. To be won to God was to enter a state of happiness which would broaden and deepen into eternal bliss. Men were to be won to this state by all that He said and did, but the great instrument of their gaining was to be the Cross. So we may say indifferently, the Son of man came to save sinners, or the Son of man came to die for sinners. How near the salvation of men was to His heart, may be seen from His whole behaviour. His rare joys rise from seeing this end in some measure accomplished. Much of the shadow of His life falls from the unbelief of men. The immense and fatal abuse of God's love and gift,—the great and affecting failures to obtain salvation,—wring from Him often cries and bursts of pain. "Many are called, but few are chosen." "Strait is the gate and narrow the way that leadeth to life, and few there be that find it."

We come next to speak of the claims of Christ. These are manifold. We select a few for comment. He claimed first of all to be equal with God. The ground on which He was condemned to die was His assertion that He was the Son of God. He claimed to be the Son of God in a unique sense, and this claim was deliberately repeated when He knew that death would be the penalty of making it. The blindest arrogance has never risen to such an audacity of blasphemy as that; for blasphemy it is if it is not truth. He claimed the attributes of God,—the power to forgive sins. In speaking to Simon the Pharisee, He claims to be the creditor to whom all debts are owing. Pharisee and Magdalene alike were in debt to Him, and by Him alone could they be forgiven. He said, "My Father worketh hitherto, and I work," thus claiming to share with the Father His world-sustaining energy. He claimed to be of one essence with the Father. "I and my Father," said He, "are one." He declared, "Before Abraham was, *I am*"; not "Before Abraham was, I was." To Nicodemus He declared Himself as the Son of God who came down from heaven, and was in heaven even while talking with him. He declared that He would ascend up where He was before. He spoke of an hour when all should hear His voice and live. He condemned the cities of Chorazin and Bethsaida for rejecting Himself. He proclaimed Himself the Emperor of the future world and the realm of the dead. He turned upon the Pharisees, and denounced them in langage which could fitly come only from the purity and power of God. He declared that He had the power of judgment, of redemption, and of fellowship with the Father.[1]

The old and awful name of God, "I Am," was taken by Jesus Christ and filled up. God revealed Himself to Moses as "I Am that I Am." Jesus says more. He takes all the symbols of strength, sufficiency, tenderness, adds them to that name, and claims it for His own. He is not only true, but He is the Truth. He is not only light, He is the Light. He is the Door, the Bread, the Water, the Good Shepherd. Whatever the human spirit can need, that He claims to supply. In Him, if His words are true, all fulness dwells. These names can be used by others only in a secondary and incomplete sense. He Himself alone can use them in the full integrity of their meaning.[2]

He invites men to come to Him, and He will give them rest. "Come unto me, all ye that labour and are heavy laden, and I will give you rest." The

---

[1] See Westcott on John, Introduction, p. 84.
[2] His claim to sinlessness will be found discussed in the concluding chapter.

words were spoken at first to a little knot of forgotten Jews, but they were made over to the weary generations of men. He confronts all the coming races with their burdens, and declares Himself able and willing to give rest to them all. Can this be the claim of a man?

Further, we notice that in His intercourse with men He claims all. He never disclaims any expression of affection and adoration as too great. It is not, "Worship God, I am of thy fellow-servants," but "Ye call me Master and Lord, and ye say well, for so I am." He claims the homage of men,—a homage as complete as can be rendered to His Father. When the woman came to Him with the box of spikenard, He did not say, "It is too much, I must not have it all," but He took it as His by right. A mere man would have said, "You are poor; it is too great a gift for your slender means." He rarely used courtesies of speech common with us: it was not His place to make requests, but to give commandments. Men were to break away at His word from the most sacred ties. Whosoever loved father or mother more than Him, was not worthy of Him. Without taking time to obey even the most pressing claims of humanity, men were at His word to follow Him. Although they did not see His ultimate intention, men were to take His plans without questioning and doubting. To doubt or question was to sin.

The immediate success or failure of His work made no difference in His self-estimate. He did not lower His claims when men left Him, nor raise them in the elation of popularity. Men came and went; He remained serenely the same. The tribute might not be rendered now, but it would be His at last. In the darkest hour of His fortunes He could calmly anticipate the time that He should be acknowledged as King of kings. Beginning His work in a peasant's garb, with almost no following, He anticipated the time when His religion should become fashionable,—when men should call Him "Lord, Lord!" and He would not know them; when His name, hardly known, or known to be despised, should become the spring of power,—the well-head of great and sweet utterances,—the name above every name, as Paul calls it,—the beautiful name, as even the stern Apostle James says, with the rare, deep tenderness of a rugged nature. Such were His claims. None other made such claims; none other claimed to stand so high, or to give so much. If these claims are untrue, can His character stand stainless? We are shut up to the old dilemma. Either He is God, or He is not good.

His divinity and humanity both appear in His claims and in His work. He was never afraid of lowering Himself. Standing on the very verge of time, with the millenniums of glory stretching on before, He paused and stooped to wash the disciples' feet. He was ready always with all the help which a man may claim from his brother. Never dazzled by earthly splendours, He was never humbled by earthly lowliness. What explanation can there be of this but the old one,—He proceeded forth and came from God?

VII
THE MIRACLES OF CHRIST

"Greater works than these shall ye do."

"Thousands of things do Thee employ
  In ruling all
This spacious globe: angels must have their joy,
  Devils their rod, the sea his shore,
The winds their stint; and yet when I did call,
  Thou heard'st my call and more."

GEORGE HERBERT.

CHAPTER VII

THE MIRACLES OF CHRIST

IT hardly accords with the plan of this work to discuss the philosophy of miracles. That miracles are possible is no question with those who believe in a personal God; that they have occurred is no question with those who believe in a divine Christ. A satisfactory philosophical foundation for miracles is to be found in the facts that God is free, and that His power is not exhausted in the creation and in the upholding of the universe. We go further, and say that miracles are probable, because the original order of the universe has been broken by sin. The perverted use of man's free will has corrupted the world, and to restore it needs the interposition of God. Christ came to restore the moral order, and in performing this miracle He had to perform many others. The end of the universe is the glory of God in the salvation of man, and everything is made to subserve that. This delivers us from being crushed by material magnitude. It supplies an answer to the question: What are we—mere specks in the immensity of things? What are we—shut in and lost amidst these frightful wastes of space which Pascal shuddered at, encompassed by flaming and unknown worlds? The reply is: We are the Church of God, which He hath purchased with His own blood. For us the course of nature exists, and if miracles are needed for our sakes they will not be refused. All that we demand about the Christian miracles is that they fulfil certain conditions. First, we may ask that they should be—not mere feats and wonders; they should have a moral meaning and end. If they are mere feats, we may suspect that they are nothing but the work of a juggler. The tricks may baffle and surprise us like many conjurers' tricks, but even although unable to explain them we shall still remain unconvinced, and declare that the worker may be nothing more than the cleverest of the host of enchanters. We shall ask that the miracles have a moral and spiritual meaning. They must be not only what they have been called, a tolling of the great bell of the universe to call the inhabitants to listen to God's sermon, but also part of the sermon. They must be not only "a great belt round the furthest sun," but also part of the sun. Further, we shall ask that these miracles be done with ease. There must be no effort and no ostentation. Man performing a miracle may be exhausted in the work, and boastful when it is accomplished. If God does it, it will be nothing to Him, for He will not rise up to it, but descend upon it. He will not have a special class of feats; He will not prepare Himself for the effort; He will not exult over the work when it is achieved. Further, He will do the work completely. The miracle will not be partial, but total. These conditions, then —first, that the miracle have a moral and spiritual end; secondly, that it be done with ease and without surprise; thirdly, that it be done completely—are conditions such as we may fairly expect to see fulfilled in the Christian miracles. We shall, after examining in detail the first miracle, and the classes into which miracles may be divided, ask how far this expectation is realised.

I.—The Beginning of Miracles

When our Lord looked over His life from the high tree of His cross, He pronounced "It is finished." By this He meant that the will of the Father had been done without defect or flaw. He was born at the right time, was silent at the right time, spoke at the right time, and in the right way wrought in deeds the perfect will of the Supreme. The more we study His life, the more we shall see that there is in it a calmness and an order, and a gentle taking up of events.

This miracle at Cana is, we are told very expressly, the beginning of miracles. Here He tolled for the first time the great bell of the universe that summoned men to listen to His sermon. We must read the miracle under that light, and when we do so we shall find that it illustrates both what went before and what was to come after in the life of Christ. The first miracle might be expected to be the least glorious. We might also hope to see in it some light thrown upon the past, and, considering how it committed Him to a divine course, we might expect to see in it how He breaks with those quiet, uneventful years. Considering also how greatly the stormy and tragic future was to differ from that peaceful past, we might expect to see how He looks forward to that future; and, besides, recognising the harmony of His life, we might expect this miracle to rule the rest, as the keynote rules the strain. These points we shall illustrate in order. First, Christ's revelation of Himself and of God was progressive. He grew up before God like a tender plant. He did not start into a sudden fulness and splendour of beauty, but had His life nurtured day by day; and so, in revealing the brightness of God, the light and the glory of His words and deeds constantly increased. So here we have a view of the mind and heart of God, as shown towards man before the stain of sin came upon the world. God, as a bountiful benefactor, here provides for His creatures' happiness. It is not good for man to be alone, and so He sanctions marriage; and as marriage is a season of gladness, He provides fit accompaniment,—provides it of the best, and in such large measure as has amazed and alarmed timid moralists. The quality and greatness of the gift were worthy of God; and we see the generosity all the more clearly, when we remember that this bountiful Creator had a little before refused to create bread to save Himself from the pangs of hunger, while here He provides wine to minister to the joy and prevent the shame of the young couple at whose nuptials He did not disdain to be present. The miracles wrought after this were for the most part miracles of healing, cures, and recoveries,—amongst these recoveries being three raisings from the dead. Had man kept pure in soul, he would have remained pure in body; but sin, which destroyed the soul, destroyed the body, and became the fruitful mother of disease and death to humanity. So, then, in these miracles we have a revelation of God showing intense sympathy with man in the distress and ruin wrought by sin. We see Him repairing the waste, and in this there is a more glorious and comforting revelation of God in His pity than we have in the first miracle, where He is revealed merely in His bounty, and where, so to speak, sin is not recognised at all. But it was at the end, when the swift eventful years of His work were past, that the most glorious revelation of God was given in miracle, when He was being led to His death,—not surrounded, as at the marriage feast, by smiling faces, but by frowning, threatening foes. One of His servants took his sword and cut off the servant of the high priest's ear. His sun was sinking into its sea, and shone brightest at its setting. "Suffer ye thus far," He said. He asked for the use of His bound hands, and, having obtained His request, He touched his ear and healed him; and though in their furious hate His enemies were all unmoved by this strange mark of love and power, —love manifested to His enemies in their supreme madness, power manifested when He seemed to be weakest,—we have leisure to mark the deed and to see the revelation which for us is highest and most welcome,—the revelation of a God showing mercy to sinners in the height of their sin. If we are ever to have mercy, we must have it as Malchus had, seeing we have had our part like him in the crucifixion of the Son of God. We see, then, in the beginning of miracles the dawn of that revelation of

God which continually waxed in brightness till the end.

Secondly, the beginning of miracles throws a light upon that past life at Nazareth with which He now broke so completely. What, we have often asked, did they do at Nazareth? How did He behave at home? Too daring imaginations of old have tried to fill the void, but in vain. We go back to the brief fragments of revelation, and are fain to content ourselves with these. But let us not neglect what we have here. Who knew His life better than His own mother? She knew that He came from God. In her heart were stored up all the mysterious revelations and manifestations of His Godhead. She had watched Him as child, boy, and man,—in His uncomplaining toil, in His constant devotion, in His true submission to the will of the Father. She had seen Him by day and night for thirty years, and she can best tell what manner of man He is. What is her testimony? "Whatsoever He saith unto you, do it." Here we have a biography in a sentence. It was as if she said, "I have watched Him all those years, and have never seen Him err. He was subject unto us, but we were gladly subject unto Him. His look commanded us, let it command you. He is born to be the leader and the commander of men. 'Whatsoever He saith unto you, do it.'" This word of His mother's lightens up strangely all the darkness of His life while He had a home. Besides, there is a very revealing glimpse into the past contained in the word *beginning*. The imaginations of men have naturally pictured these

Nazareth years as full of wonders. But it was not so. There was no miracle till the hour struck, and God's hour did not strike till now. The miracle at Cana was the beginning of miracles.

Thirdly, that past there is over, and, as we might expect, we see here how He breaks with it. "What have I to do with thee?" He says to His mother. After all the attempts that have been made to soften the apparent harshness of this speech, it remains true that there is something in it—as there is in the subsequent record of His relations with His mother—which cannot be explained unless we remember that Jesus was the Son of God. He was subject unto her before, but now the fleshly ties were broken—He was obedient no more; a higher voice called Him, and He must go. It was part of the cross of Christ, as it has been part of the cross of many of His people, that the work of God severed His earthly ties. His mother must have been exceptionally near and dear to Him. That loving heart could not but have clung to the companions of early years. It could not but have been a pang to Him to repel His mother's advances and remonstrances in His public work. Even we are touched with the patient fidelity that clung to Him, and refused to believe in the rebuffs or to accept the fact that the old tie of mother and son was broken. Few words of the Bible go so straight to the heart as those which tell that there was by the cross of Jesus His mother, clinging to the last, present with Him in His last agony, the pain of which, if in one way it might have been lightened, was in another way increased by the anguish of her look. He had to tell her—He does tell her here—that the earthly bonds exist no more; that others may come as near Him as she; that whosoever shall do the will of God, the same is His brother, and sister, and mother.

We seem to perceive here not only a backward look on the past, but also a look to the future. "What have I to do with thee? Mine hour is not yet come." These last words have perplexed interpreters so much, that a recent writer says they cannot be explained either by Protestants or Roman Catholics.[1] But may we not see in it something of the feeling of one who was Himself about to take a decisive step from a life of peace into a life of conflict and gloom that was to darken into death? Is it not the cry of a sleeper awakened on the morning of a day which is to end in a terrible tragedy? Surely, He says, the day is not yet come; surely there are some hours to run before it begins. So Jesus shrank as He opened His eyes on the grey and awful dawn of that day, whereof the midnight was to be so black and all the hours so bitter. He had loved Nazareth. He had been happy in the holy and beautiful morning of His life. The name Jesus of Nazareth, which His foes hammered over His dying head, was a name He never was ashamed of. It was the name He used long after, when He spoke out of heaven to Saul lying blind on the dazzling road. He had loved the journey on the smooth sward, and now it had come to an end; and He sees before Him the road of flints, at every step of

[1] Dr. W. G. Ward in his Essays. See Note D.

which His blood will run. So He shrinks back for the moment: "Mine hour is not yet come." But instantly He recalls Himself, and goes on to the work.

> "What is it thou buriest so softly and still?—
> Oh, this is the grave of my own proud will:
> I bid it sleep softly in this little room,
> And my hopes, too, I bury with it in the tomb."

He had no proud, rebellious will to break and bury, and yet there was a struggle. In this passion before the Passion we see that shrinking which we often trace later, and at the same time that stedfast purpose which mastered it, and carried Him on to the decease that He should accomplish at Jerusalem. So He put His hand to the work. The bell was rung for the first time, and He never drew back.

Then, lastly, this miracle rules the rest, as the keynote rules the strain. He manifested His glory. There was also a revelation of the glory of God; but the miracles of Christ were singular in this respect, that they manifested His glory. Moses manifested God's glory, and sinned when he forgot that that was all he could do; but the miracles of Christ are all expressions and revelations of His own glory. We see in them His heart, His power, His will to work and to suffer for our sakes. The revelation made at the beginning is, as we shall see, continued through the rest. Having regard to the symbolic character of John's Gospel, we can hardly err in seeing here besides a sign of the nature of the work of Christ, which was to take natural homely things and enrich and transfigure them. His work was to turn the water of earth into the wine of heaven.

We thus perceive that in the beginning of miracles there is the beginning of a revelation of God. There is a light thrown on the Saviour's past, there is a breaking with that past, there is a forward looking to the future, and there is the keynote given which was to rule the miracles that were to come.

II.—The Kinds of Miracles

The miracles of Christ are a complete revealing of His power and nature, so far as everything known to man is concerned. We find them including examples of His power over nature, His power over external objects, His power over man's bodily frame, His power over man's mind, His power over death and him that hath the power of death, that is, the devil.

1. His power over external nature is illustrated by His stilling the waves of the sea. On one occasion He was with His disciples crossing the stormy Sea of Galilee, and in the hinder part of the ship He was sleeping on the pillow. He had not where to lay His head. But the weary head is not hard to please with a pillow, and He was very weary. The sleep of the labouring man is sweet, and He was sleeping the sleep of one wearied in teaching, and helping, and saving man,—a heavy, dreamless slumber, undisturbed by the tumult of wind and waves. The disciples did not waken Him till the last moment. They waited as long as they could. "The ship was filling," says one evangelist, giving the view of one on board. "It was

now covered with the waves," says another, describing it as seen by somebody standing on the shore. But when it came to that, they turned to Him, saying, "Master, carest thou not that we perish?" Two things were contending,—on the one hand trust, and on the other the old world-nature. But the trust was uppermost, for they came to Him, saying, "Master." We are all equal up to a certain point. For a time there is no difference between us, but in great crises of life the deliverer is sought out and found in a moment. It was an impossible thing that He should not care for their perishing, and so their fears and their faith drove them to the stern where the sleeping Christ was lying. That cry—half faith, half fear—brought Him to His feet; and He made answer, "Why are ye fearful, O ye of little faith?" His calm soul brought calm. He rebuked the wind, and said unto the sea, "Peace, be still." His word produced an instant effect on the tumult outside. There was a great calm. After a storm comes a swell; after this storm came a calm. And with what perfect ease was the miracle wrought! The wearied Man who had laid Himself down to rest rouses Himself up, awakened by the complaint of the disciples, and in a moment tames and subdues the power of nature. The two thoughts coupled together —of the sleeping Christ and the awakened Christ—give us the image and thought of Him in whom we trust, with all the weakness of humanity that brings us so near Him, and at the same time with all the great power of God.

2. His power over external objects is illustrated by the miracle already discussed, the turning of water into

wine. It appears also in that miracle which excited so great a commotion, and which He made the text of His sermon on the bread of life—The Feeding of the Five Thousand. This is the one miracle narrated by all four evangelists. The multitude had assembled, pressing upon Jesus. He had sought quiet, but they would not allow Him to find it. After preaching to them, Jesus had compassion upon their necessities, and asked the disciples whence bread could be procured that they might eat. A lad had four barley loaves and two fishes, barley loaves being the ordinary black bread of the Galilean peasants. But what were they among so many? They confessed themselves baffled by so great a difficulty, and so Jesus commanded the disciples to arrange the people in ranks upon the grass. The miracle must have occurred early in the year, for in that country the grass is burnt and brown before the end of April. That so huge a multitude should have arranged themselves so obediently, shows that they had that faith without which, in all likelihood, the miracle would not have been wrought. They ranged themselves rank after rank. And what expectancy there must have been as the order was gradually formed, and Christ faced them calmly with the slight provision He was so marvellously to multiply! They were seated on the grass like rows of flowers, to use the picturesque word of one of the evangelists,—which refers probably to their bright Eastern dresses,[1]—all gazing wistfully, and expecting they knew not what. Often men have to prepare when there is no sign of anything,—to dig ditches for the rain beneath a blue,

[1] Καὶ ἀνέπεσον πρασιαὶ πρασιαί, Mark vi. 40.

blazing sky, to build barns for a harvest not begun to grow. So it was here. He faced them with no dismay,—with a great pity, and the full consciousness that He had power to indulge that pity. So, when all was ready, the bread was broken and distributed to the multitude. All had a share; and after all were provided there was a surplus, which was carefully gathered for future needs. This miracle produced a deep impression, and roused the people to enthusiasm, inducing them to resolve to crown Him as their king. This miracle—in some respects the most remarkable of all in the Gospels, one which modern theorists find particularly refractory—shows not only the ease and completeness with which Christ could perform His miracles, but also the reserve, the economy, with which He used His power. Though a word created all that vast store, the fragments had to be gathered so that nothing should be lost. It was but seldom that Christ miraculously afforded provision for man's physical necessities; and the reason doubtless is, that He feared to corrupt them by putting them beyond the need of honest labour. Indiscriminate charity has done much to demoralise the poor; but His charity was carefully accommodated to their actual necessities and their true welfare.

3. Most of His miracles manifested His power over man's bodily frame. He healed diseases. Diseases, frequently of repulsive form, were common then in Palestine, and the Healer had brought to Him crowds of sufferers, none of whom came in vain. So pressing were the claims of the sick and their importunate friends, that He had often to tell those who were

healed not to spread the news abroad. His miracles of healing were often performed on leprosy. Leprosy was a type of sin, and it is notable that He never paused when a leper cried to Him. He gave also recovery of sight to them that were blind. Blindness, as now, was sadly common in Eastern lands. He healed those who were sick of the fever, and His healing left them not weak and weary, but strong and vigorous. The main points to be noticed in His treatment of disease are such as these: He was no specialist —every class of disease was amenable to His will; He never had to ask for time or for helps; before seeing the disease He undertook to cure it; His cures were never gradual recoveries—they were always complete.

4. His power over man's mind is shown by His knowledge of what was in man. From the beginning He knew who should betray Him. When Nathanael was under the fig tree He saw him; when Simon was cherishing the uncharitable thought in his heart, He knew what was passing in his mind. Naked and open were all men to the eyes of Him with whom they had to do.

5. His sovereignty over death was manifested three times, as well as in His own resurrection. He raised Jairus' daughter, the widow's son, and Lazarus. These three times are, so far as we know, the only occasions in which He ever came in contact with death. Jairus' daughter was just dead, the widow's son was being carried to his grave a few hours after death, Lazarus was dead four days. But these differences were nothing. With equal ease they were all called forth and restored to their old life. Their restoration was in

each case out of sympathy for those who bewailed their loss. Jairus, the ruler of the synagogue, rushed out from the house where his little daughter lay at the point of death, and broke in on Christ seated with the publicans and sinners at the table of that despised one whom probably Jairus had himself scourged out of the synagogue. He made his appeal, and the Master went with him like a servant. Their journey to the house was broken by the woman who touched the hem of His garment and was made whole. And when they reached the house, Jairus' daughter was gone. But He said, "She is not dead, but sleepeth." It was not His manner to magnify His miracles. He did not say, "She is sevenfold dead," but, "She sleepeth." And with tender words He called her from her short slumber. When He saw the widowed mother weeping for her only son, He had compassion on her, and touched the bier, and said, "Young man, I say to thee, Arise." When He came to the grave of Lazarus, his friend, and saw the two sisters whom He loved deep in grief, and the company of the Jews weeping with them, His heart was moved with trouble and anger at the victory of sin, and in pure sympathy for their tears he wept, and cried, "Lazarus, come forth." His cheeks were wet with the tears of sympathy, and yet His word was shot into the darkness of the tomb and the dull cold ear of Death, and he who had been dead came forth in his grave-clothes with shrouded face. As Augustine says remarkably, "He calls him by name, lest He should bring forth all the dead." In each of these cases He completes the miracle. He is not flushed or agitated by His triumph. As soon as the dead man sits up and begins to speak, He delivers him to his mother. When the young maiden is raised, with delicate consideration He commands that something shall be given her to eat. When He sees the bound face and feet and hands of Lazarus, He reminds those who stand by petrified with astonishment to loose him and let him go. He does all things beautifully well.[1]

6. His power is shown also over him that hath the power of death, that is, the devil. There were diseases in the time of Christ which were solemnly attributed by their Healer to the power of unclean spirits. Evil at that time was permitted to manifest itself with terrible distinctness, that it might be met by the mightiest manifestation of good. He conquered in every case where He encountered it. One case, decidedly the most terrible of all, may be referred to. A man who had been long possessed, who wore no clothes, and dwelt in no house, but abode in the tombs, cried out when he saw Jesus, "What have I to do with Thee, Thou Son of God most high?" There was something in the look of Christ that was troubling the hidden devils. He expelled them, and the man out of whom the devils departed sat at the feet of Jesus, clothed and in his right mind. Beautiful in its suffused calm is this picture of the restored man, when it is put in contrast with the paroxysm of madness and misery from which he had been delivered. He was sitting. That was wonderful, for the terrible restlessness of his malady had made him incapable of a moment's rest. Now the tension has collapsed. He is master of himself, sitting. He is clothed. Chains could not hold him before, but

[1] Καλῶς, Mark vii. 37.

now he is restored to a consciousness of the decencies of life. And the explanation of it all is that he is at the feet of Jesus. Jesus has brought him into quiet, and sanity, and decency; and the man, in strange contrast with those who prayed that Christ would depart out of their coasts, implores Him that he may be with Him, lest the old evil power should surge over his spirit once more.

These narratives and the rest seem to satisfy all the conditions which we may lawfully demand in the miracles of Christ. They are done with infinite ease, with an exuberance of power. They are not great efforts, but repeated again and again. There is no sign of exhaustion. The multitude are astonished, but He is not astonished. Then they are not done recklessly or lawlessly. While there is great ease there is great reserve, and every particle of power is accounted for. When the woman touches Him, He knows that virtue has gone out of Him, and demands who it was that drew Him. Again, the miracles are complete. Nothing has to be added to them—no one can amend them. And they are all pregnant with revelations of God's nature and purposes. Some are, in all probability, symbolical of definite spiritual truths; all are distinct revelations of the mind and heart of God. This being so, we are justified in placing them on a different platform from all other miracles.

He Himself never rated His miracles highly. "Greater works than these shall ye do," He said to His disciples. But He never said, "Greater words than these shall ye speak," or "Greater thoughts than these shall ye think." He knew that the needs supplied for the moment would recur, that the sicknesses would come back worse, and that the bitterness of death was not past. But it was natural that He should do miracles. Would He have been God manifest in the flesh if He had journeyed deaf, and bound, and helpless through the evils and distresses of humanity? This was impossible, and therefore miracles were done. But signs and idle wonders He indignantly declined to perform. Of works of mercy there was a plenitude, but He refused to work wonders which would merely gratify a vacant or transient curiosity. To create belief, not to raise astonishment, was His object; and the works He did were enough to make unbelief without excuse.

It is incomplete to say that the miracles justify belief in Christ, and it is equally incomplete to say that it is belief in Christ that makes miracles credible. Christ comes before us as a whole—His person and His work. It is impossible to separate the two, and we believe in the whole—that is, in both.

VIII
THE TEACHING OF CHRIST

"Never man spake like this Man."

"O holy Truth, whene'er thy voice is heard,
  A thousand echoes answer to the call;
Though oft inaudible thy gentle word,
  While we regard not. Take me from the thrall
Of passionate Hopes, be thou my all in all;
  So may Obedience lead me by the hand
Into thine inner shrine and secret hall."

ISAAC WILLIAMS.

CHAPTER VIII

THE TEACHING OF CHRIST

A POINT always noticed by our Lord's hearers was, that His teaching differed from that of all others: "Never man spake like this Man." He spoke like a man, and yet no man ever spoke like Him. The criticism of those who left Him after hearing one of His sermons was, "Not as the Scribes." Whether the teaching was good or evil they might not be able to say, but of this at least they were sure, that it was different from the teaching they had been accustomed to hear.

The double thread of divinity and humanity is to be traced also in the teaching of Christ.

He spake with authority. It was this that first struck the people as marking Him out as different from the Scribes. The Scribes always made appeals to others. They quoted traditional interpretations, and sought to win the assent of their hearers by appealing to those who had gone before. But Jesus appealed to His own authority: "*I* say unto you." The Scribes were aware of the opposition their statements might excite, and of the silent resistance with which men are always prone to meet any unfamiliar truth, and they took the usual means to anticipate and master that resistance. They employed authority, argument; and if these failed, the fortress might be captured by appeals to passion. But with Jesus it was different. He appealed to no prejudice; He made no concession to passion. He spoke as one who knew that He possessed the truth, and that the truth had a welcome prepared for it from of old within obedient hearts. For the most part He did not argue; and although it is true that an Eastern discourse is generally a collection of loosely connected sayings, resembling in its entirety not a living organism, but a heap of jewels, each beautiful in itself, and that this is so with Christ's, yet that is not the whole. When He says, "Believe in me," "Follow me," "I am the truth," "Verily, verily, I say unto you," He is speaking with the sublime certainty of one who knows that, as a divine teacher, He has a right to the empire and assent of every soul of man. It is true that He refers to the Bible; but in His references He, as it were, stands above it, and sets His seal upon it, even when He has claimed its sanction for His own words. The prophets effaced themselves by appealing to God, whose witnesses they were, and prefaced their words by "Thus saith the Lord." He spoke the most startling truths, and offered no certificate but that of His own authority. And as He was the authoritative teacher, so He was the commander of men. He never gave advice. He did not say, "If you please": His words were imperative; they were law; they were guarded by the most awful sanctions; to disobey them was to incur the risk of eternal ruin. The difference between law and advice is one appreciable measure of the difference between Christ and human teachers. This was what men needed then, and need now. Those who believed in Him first were weary of debating; they were not sure of their own power to thread labyrinths of reasoning, or resist appeals to passion, and they craved for a solid foundation on which they might build the hopes that were dear as life. So it is still. In the time of health and prosperity, men may delight in speculation and inquiry; but when the great shocks and overthrows of life come, men seek something that will uphold them, that will enlighten them as to what lies beyond the deep darkness of the grave. The search for truth, so fascinating once, becomes weary when men have little time and no heart to pursue it, and the eternal realities are near. Then the truth itself is sought,—the truth that knows its responsibilities, its frontiers, its consequences. Doubts only make a man impatient, while he is met and satisfied by the vast claims of Him who asserted that Himself was the Christ. Instead of chafing at the immense assumption involved, he is thankful then that the words of Christ are so calmly assumed, so sublimely imperative. Yet Jesus spoke as a man, for with all these claims He fell back upon God's word. He did not profess to be able to dispense with it, but fed upon it, put His trust in it, and drank out of it as from an ever-living spring.

He spoke with full and intimate knowledge of the ways of men, and yet as one who was entirely above them. His parables are full of proofs that He had observed human work and ways with a close and kindly scrutiny. The woman putting the leaven into the meal, the children playing in the market-place, the sower sowing the seed,—these and many other homely scenes of life did not escape Him. He knew human nature thoroughly in all its best and worst phases. A singular illustration of this is His story of the two sons, or, as it is usually called, the story of the Prodigal Son. How, we ask, will one who has never known wickedness, whose mind has never been sullied, whose lips have never been polluted by any drop of the cup of evil, understand the bitter and tortuous ways of sin? How will He, who has hardly been away from His mother's side, describe the course of one who has left his home and gone to the far country, and wasted there his substance with riotous living? Let this story answer. With what supreme truth the whole miserable history is told. There are two sons, and it is the younger son, who had latest received the ministries of love, who first forgets them. Indulged, probably, he wearies even of the golden chains, and asks for his portion, gathers all together, and takes his journey into a far country. He gathers all together, for he has no thought of return; and he takes his journey into a far country, for his idea of happiness is to be as remote from his father as possible. For a time all goes well; but when the money is spent, a mighty famine arises in the land. Can we be wrong in thinking that there is a reference here to the mighty famine which a prodigal who has spent all his money always finds around him? So long as he was rich, doors and purses were open to him. But whenever he came to want, those who had helped him to scatter his father's savings had nothing to give him. No man gave unto him. The most terrible indictment of human nature ever written. And yet nature's sternest painter is the best. These were no true friends—only boon companions; and so he is driven in his despair to an occupation the very mention of which would have sent a shudder through our Lord's hearers. He was sent into the fields to feed swine. And then, in his dire extremity, he turned fatherwards and homewards. Or rather, it was not his father he saw, but the well-provisioned house,—the house where even the hired servants had bread enough and to spare. The bare fields and the stripped trees look drearier than ever, and he says, "I will be done with all this." And he rises, remembering that he is not worthy of the least mercy. He frames his confession; and what tears, what burning shame there are in it: "Father, I have sinned against Heaven, and in thy sight, and am no more worthy to be called thy son: make me as one of thy hired servants." The speech is never uttered; it is cut in twain by a great burst of forgiving love. His father runs to meet him, kisses his trembling lips into silence, seats him at the board, and the house rings with welcome, because the dead is living, and the lost is found. And with what a sure hand does our Lord describe what may be called the respectable vices! He understands profligacy and the grosser forms of sin, but the picture of the elder brother, with its delicate touches, shows that He understood sins less recognised, but as deadly. Every word tells. When the elder brother sees the red lights flushing the window, and hears the unwonted joy, he begins his complaint without saying "Father." He speaks of his *many* years of servitude as one for whom the time had moved with leaden feet. "Neither transgressed I at any time thy commandments,"—one who had given a loveless obedience, but no more. "Thou never gavest me a kid, that I might make merry with my friends,"—an unloving soul that had never called forth any warm token of love. "Thy son who hath devoured his living with harlots,"—a hasty and uncharitable inference. And the same patient love includes and forgives the two. It is a humbling fact, that men who have proclaimed God's truth with great results have been themselves full of envy, jealousy,—have known the conflict of the worst passions, and have too often yielded to their power. The very fact of their knowing these malign emotions, the experimental evidence that they were struggling with them, has made them better able to speak to men like-minded, than those cast in another mould, whose souls have been less vexed with these stormy winds. And yet the fact that they have yielded to sin has weakened and almost paralysed them while denouncing it. Jesus combined the two things,—perfect knowledge of sin, and perfect freedom from sin,—and therefore spoke with double power. He never illustrates from His own life, but finds weapons to pierce the conscience in the history of human hearts, whose baseness He knew to the very uttermost.

He observed external nature, and said exquisite things about it. His calm eyes saw through the pretence and gaudiness of man's attempts at decoration, and He said of the quiet lilies in the field, that Solomon in all his glory was not arrayed like one of these. Yet He did not linger upon nature lovingly, as many of our poets have done. It would not be correct to say, with Dr. Watts, that "He glides along by mortal things without a thought of love"; but we need not be afraid to speak of His admiration for nature, for His glances at nature, though heedful, are not close and passionate. He speaks as one who stands far above it, whose eyes are familiar with far fairer scenes. He is utterly above the prejudices both of rich and poor. The poor had the gospel preached to them. He went about amidst the villages and lanes of Galilee doing justice to their long-neglected claims, but He did nothing unworthy to win favour amongst them. He held out to them no prospect of earthly reward, and His way of giving happiness to them was very different from what they imagined. He was the Christ of the people, not in the democratic sense of selecting a particular class for His favour, for His message was one meant as much for the rich as for the poor. He never sought to gain the rich, and indeed went counter to all the views current amongst them. In short, He was far above rich and poor alike,—far above the whole atmosphere of His time. We feel that all His words are spoken from a commanding standpoint,—from an elevation to which no mere man can ever climb; and yet with all this they show the clearest intelligence of man's ways and needs, as well as the closest sympathy.

His teaching was new, and yet it attached itself to all truth that had been revealed before. It was original. Nothing has been more distinctly brought out by recent investigation, than the absolute originality of our Lord's teaching. The few and remote analogies that have been discovered with the teaching of the day, have only served to present this in a clearer light. But He was not original in the sense of being destructive. His teaching was not built upon the ruins of old systems. It is easy to destroy, hard to build, but most difficult to develop. The last was His work. He took the law and precepts of the old Jewish religion, set up His new divine ideal of conduct, and connected the two. He declared that not one jot or tittle of the law should fail; that He came not to destroy but to fulfil; and set Himself, especially in the Sermon on the Mount, to show how His teaching attached itself to and transcended Old Testament teaching. He took the commandments, affirmed them, and explained that they related not merely to acts, but to desires. He carried them into regions of which the old law knew nothing. Going beyond the highest reach of human wisdom, He declared that men were to love one another as He had loved them. He overturned the traditional maxims, which had in society more force perhaps than the laws of God, and declared that what was highly esteemed among men was abominable in the eyes of God. In short, He undertook the most difficult of all tasks,—to meet the people upon a common platform, and to lift them up by showing that His teaching, while new, was yet a true development of the old revelation of God.

His teaching was characterised at once by simplicity and profundity. His sayings were simple in form,—so much so that the common people heard Him gladly. They felt that they understood what He had said, and wished to hear more. But soon they perceived that there was more in these sayings than they had imagined. They had another meaning and another, and seemed to grow deeper with deepening life. They were like clear wells, into which one may gaze without seeing the bottom. They were like sea-shells sounding with the immeasurable depth. Every word had in it the echo of eternity. Or, to use another illustration, they were like that bread which appeared scarcely sufficient for a few, and yet sufficed for five thousand, with a large provision left over. These words of Christ have in them the infinitude of Godhead; and the years that have passed since they were spoken have been spent in developing their meaning. Yet, as one of their deepest students has declared, we are only on the outskirts of the knowledge of them. The bread has been broken amongst men and has sufficed, and still there is more. The teaching of Christ was not exhaustive but germinant,—like a handful of seeds and roots, with great possibilities which have never been unfolded; which never will be, because they are infinite. No other chief of thought has this depth, this influence. Every other teacher comes to be criticised and questioned, every other master has his place filled, but a willing Christendom still sits at the feet of Christ.

Again, His words are remarkable for their intellectual qualities, and at the same time never marked by mere cleverness. He never needed to meditate before He gave an answer; and, as we shall see, most of His finest sayings were struck from Him in the heat of argument. He could make sharp retorts and replies, but He seldom cared to do so. He never was disingenuous,—never escaped by a quirk or quibble. His sayings were all perfect in their form. His diction is not an artificial fold which may be taken off His thoughts and replaced by another. The thought lives through every particle of the style. To cut is to wound.[1] Yet of form there was no apparent thought; and all was spoken not to display the gift of the speaker, but to win the hearts of the hearers. He Himself paid absolutely no regard to intellectual eminence. His disciples were not amongst the wise and prudent, and He was thankful that it was so. He did not indeed disparage study and learning; but His criterion of judgment was not the criterion of the schools, and nothing was of any account in His eyes save what made for the purity and simplicity of the soul. He had no intellectual pride; and though He could have held the whole Sanhedrim in audience, and commanded the admiration of the learned, He never made the attempt.

He speaks of heaven, of the future world, as a witness. Yet all His revelation is carefully shaded to make it fit for our eyes. He claims to know the Father as none other can. He knows the interior relations of the Godhead. He beheld Satan as lightning fall from heaven, and knows of the joy that is in the presence

[1] A perusal of the well-intentioned modern travesties of Christ's words is instructive. See Foster's *Journal*, 393.

of the angels of God over one sinner that repenteth. He is familiar with the many mansions in His Father's house, and speaks of departing to prepare a place there for His disciples. Speaking to Nicodemus, He forgets the narrow street, with the wind moaning along it, and says, "The Son of man which is in heaven." Yet how little is spoken, how many pressing questions are left unanswered! Not because He could not answer them, for this reticence goes along with clear, calm, confident knowledge. It was not that He did not know; it was because the knowledge was too high and too deep to be expressed to men.

Such are some of the characteristics of Christ's teaching. Into the matter of that teaching we do not enter at present. Of this teaching He said Himself that it would last longer than heaven and earth. Yet He took none of the ordinary precautions for the preservation of His teaching. He never wrote, except once upon the ground. His method, however, was more effectual, for He put His law in the mind, and wrote it on the heart,[1] and the two thousand years that have gone past have never as yet given the lie to His saying. Many a name has risen and set since then. Many words have been spoken and forgotten; but never since they were uttered first have the words of Christ been more earnestly heeded and studied than they are to-day. There are voices that tell us that these words also will pass away, and that the influence of Christ will decay, as has decayed the influence of other teachers. But what is to take their place? They fill

[1] See Aquinas, *Summa*, Quæst. 42, Art. 4.

a void which must be filled, and which no other words do anything to supply. They are living and mighty still; and until we see other words likely to be their substitute, we prefer to believe that He spoke but the sober truth when He said that they would endure when heaven and earth had passed away.

IX

THE APOSTLES OF CHRIST

"**Ye are they which have continued with me in my temptations.**"

"We were weary, and we
Feeble and faint in our march,
Ready to drop down and die;
Still thou turnedst, and still
Beckon'dst the trembler, and still
Gavest the weary thine hand.
If in the ways of the world
Stones have wounded thy feet,
Toil or dejection have tried
Thy spirit, of that we saw
Nothing; to us thou wert still
Cheerful and helpful and firm.
Thus to thee it was given
Many to save with thyself,
And at the end of the day,
O faithful Shepherd, to come,
Bringing thy sheep in thy hand."

M. ARNOLD.

CHAPTER IX

THE APOSTLES

SOME of the apostles were at first disciples of John, —probably all were so,—and this fact shows that they were men of moral earnestness, wearied of the unsatisfying religion that was in vogue, and needing something more. They were men also who could not rest under the preliminary dispensation of John, and who eagerly embraced the Messiah when He appeared. At first their faith was not mature. Although they saw in Christ the fulfilment of Old Testament prophecy, that prophecy they interpreted in a very carnal and unworthy sense. Still they were enthusiasts. They had the root of the matter in them, and He who measured them exactly from the first saw their fitness for their place.

At first they appeared to have been only occasional companions of Christ. We find them, for example, with Jesus at His first miracle, wrought at the marriage at Cana. Then they began to attend on His person, and to be with Him almost without a break, accompanying Him in His preaching journeys throughout the land. Their function was to be eyewitnesses and ministers of the word; and in order that nothing should be lost, it was needful that He should soon have about Him a company of disciples. After a time He chose twelve of them as apostles, partly to be free of the inconvenient crowd that pursued His steps, but mainly for two reasons,—first, that they might be with Him; and, secondly, that they might be fishers of men. The number twelve had reference no doubt to the twelve tribes of Israel, besides its convenience otherwise. The twelve apostles were chosen at least a year before His crucifixion. We do not know very much of the greater part of them. They were poor men chosen from the lower classes, partly because the wise and prudent did not give ear to Christ, partly because there was less misapprehension in their minds to combat. Two or three of them were men of singular gifts,—in particular, John and Peter. John was the disciple whom Jesus specially loved, the disciple who understood best His soul and His object. Of John we have a tolerably complete portraiture in the Gospels. He was a man of fiery, vigorous character externally, but underneath the apparent force and impulse there was a great and gentle love,—a love that was a profound intelligence, making him fit to gaze on God's greatest revelations. Some difficulty has been felt in harmonising the two ideas,—the Son of Thunder and the Apostle of Love. It has been suggested that as years grew, and as the Master's influence was more felt, the fiery passions of youth were cooled. One advocate of this view says: "It is a tribute to the power of Christ, that He subdued and dominated such a nature. A traveller, giving an account of an ancient volcano which he visited, tells of a wondrous cup-like hollow on the mountain summit, and where the fierce heat had once burned, a still, clear pool of water looking up like an eye to the beautiful heavens above." But the difficulty of imagining the two together has perhaps been exaggerated. The great deeps of his nature were unmoved, though the surface might be vexed with transient storm. Peter's character is more easily comprehended. A hasty, audacious, impulsive temperament, a warm heart, strong common sense,—these were his main characteristics. Christ discerned from the first the genuine worth of the man, and called him a man of rock. The features of his life are all in keeping, and are, as it were, echoes of the central one,—his denial of the Lord. One time he saw Christ in the sea through the uncertain glimpses of the stormy moonlight, longed to be near to Him, and stepped over the boat to walk to Him on the water. But when he felt the spray in his face, and the unevenness of the waves' flow, his faith and courage failed him. So at the end he avowed that though all men should forsake Christ he would not—he would die for Him. His imagination, however, had conceived the result but not the process. He had overestimated his own strength. The cold of the day, the want of sleep, the jeers of the servant girl,—these and other little things came together and mastered him, so that he denied the Lord, and having once denied Him, his iniquity, like the wind, took him away. He denied Him a second and a third time, with oaths and curses. The two disciples sometimes appear together. Peter and John, after the resurrection, go together to the tomb. John stands outside, but Peter makes his way in. And again, when they see Christ upon the shore,

Peter's eagerness will not allow him to wait till they have crossed the little strip of water that is between them and Him; he casts himself into the sea, and, half wading, half swimming, he makes his way to the feet of his thrice-denied Lord, while John waits till he has reached the shore. Thomas has been called the Paley of the apostles, from his desire to have verified to him experimentally the fact that Christ had risen. The term is not felicitous, for Thomas had little in common with Paley, and as little in common with the sceptics of the nineteenth century. These strange alternations of cold doubt and passionate affection, which appear in the few recorded incidents of Thomas' life, separate him from most doubters. He had a warm heart, but a melancholy temperament, and his fears and doubts were often too strong for his faith, though not for his love. We have a definite impression of some of the other apostles; of others we know little. And "we must learn to think of them not as exceptionally gifted and holy men, but as very like the honest, hard-featured men we may see standing in a knot at the corner of any fishing village, or at whose superstitious legends or domestic tales or ignorant questions we may laugh when we spend a night with them in their boat." Our Lord trained these twelve. They had the inestimable privilege of going in and out with Him. They were trained by what they heard and by what they saw. They had His direct influence as well as the indirect. A large part of His life and effort was devoted to their instruction. To them was communicated a great part of the Lord's teaching that they might deliver it. What they heard in the darkness they were to speak in the light; what was spoken to them in the ear was to be declared on the house-tops. Their patient Master had to contend with much ignorance, narrowness, and superstition on their part; but there was true devotion to Him, and that devotion did in the end prove victorious over all that impeded it. He gently accommodated His revelation to their minds. He taught them as they were able to bear it. His hardest task was to disabuse them of their carnal idea of the Messianic kingdom. At last, when they seemed in a measure ready for it, He showed them that He had to die. They came to a turn in the road from which the end might be seen. They looked forward and saw in the distance—what? Not thrones in Jerusalem where they were to sit by His side as temporal princes, but the great cross on which the Son of man must be lifted up.

The decisive interview, which forms such a turning-point in the Gospels, is carefully described. "Whom say men that I am?" He asked them first. They gave Him for reply: "Some say, Elias; others, One of the old prophets,"—perhaps with some instinctive delicacy concealing from Him the worst that was said. He appealed from this judgment of the outer circle to them who knew Him better: "Whom say ye that I am?" And may we not say that He waited with anxiety for the answer,—an answer that would show the result of all His training and example? It came full of music and truth from the lips of Peter: "Thou art the Christ, the Son of the living God." "Blessed art thou," He said with quick gladness; "flesh and blood hath not revealed it unto thee, but my Father which is in heaven." Having thus established them in the faith of His person, He begins to unfold the future. Just as men find it needful often to prepare their fellows for the announcement of hard tidings, by establishing them in the assurance that it is a friend who speaks, so He wished them to understand who He was, that they might be able to accept the revelation that was coming. "The Son of man must go to Jerusalem, and suffer many things of the elders and chief priests and scribes, and be killed, and be raised again the third day." It is not of a probability that He speaks. He does not say, "The anger of my foes is increasing, and may soon end in a storm which will destroy me." He spoke of a certainty which must be. He "must go to Jerusalem"—that of itself was bad news—"and suffer many things"—the picture grows darker—"and be killed"—that is midnight. And then He shoots a bar of light across it and makes it all clear—"and be raised again the third day." But they did not hear Him out; they heard about the death, but no further. Peter took Him and began to rebuke Him. "Be it far from thee, Lord: this shall not be unto thee." If there had been any hesitation in His mind, this was the time to bring it forth. The heart grows faint sometimes, when a great purpose, as it were, takes shape in words. The eyes are dazzled, and a very little would make the resolve collapse. But it is not so here. "Get thee behind me, Satan"; for He hears again the voice that in the wilderness sought to tempt Him by pointing a short way to the kingdom. "Thou savourest not the things that be of God, but those that are of men." Then He goes on and tells all:—The law of His kingdom was cross-bearing. His disciples had each to bear a cross. He that saved his life would lose it; he that lost his life for Christ's sake would find it. There was a day coming when the wisdom of following Him even with a cross and to a cross would be manifest to all. The sluice is lifted now, and He talks freely, as we ourselves have found it easy to say much that had been long pent up, when the difficult first word was spoken. So far as there is record, He is not interrupted further, for the disciples had more difficulty with the thought that He had to bear a cross, than with the thought that they themselves had to bear it. Even when the solemn end came, when the great depths of His heart were broken up, His purpose with these disciples seemed very imperfectly achieved. They could not keep awake by Him in Gethsemane; they nearly all forsook Him at the cross. Peter himself denied Him thrice. After His death they all scattered, but after the resurrection He gathered them again, and gave them the great charge to go everywhere preaching the gospel: "Lo, I am with you alway, even to the end of the world."

The disciples were chosen, first, that they might be with Christ. He had a real gladness and strength in their companionship. There is a note of pain when He says, "The hour cometh when ye shall be scattered every man to his own, and shall leave me alone." In the supreme crisis of His agony He longs to know that the human companionship was near. To be utterly forsaken was a deep grief. "I looked for some to pity, but there was none, and for comforters, but I found none." When they failed to give Him their company, He reproaches them gently: "Could ye not watch with me one hour?" He is grateful even for their uncomprehending fellowship. "Ye are they," says He, "who have continued with me in my temptations." He knew the denials and unbelief that were coming; He knew their partial sympathy and knowledge: and yet He was thankful even for their poor company, for their wavering affection, for their doubting faith, and their self-willed submission. And yet, thankful though He is for their presence, and even in a sense dependent upon it, He does not lean on them as the strongest man is often thankful to lean upon his weakest brother. Never does He take counsel with them; never does He pray along with them as a man with his brothers: He always stands, while near them, yet infinitely apart.

But they were chosen chiefly to be instruments in carrying on the work of His kingdom. Before He ordained the twelve apostles He had been in prayer, and had commanded them to pray the Lord of the harvest to thrust forth more labourers into His harvest. He put it into their hearts, as it were, to answer their own prayer by making themselves labourers. He gave them power. Who was this that could distribute the omnipotence of God? He was not weakened by this bestowal of power, but remained as rich as ever. Who was this that always gave and never received, and yet was not exhausted? The power was beneficent to heal, to cast out devils. It was easily appreciated, yet it was strictly limited. The apostles were nothing in themselves: all that they had was His gift, and was meant to show forth His glory.

We cannot read the Bible carefully without feeling

that the view it takes of God's workers is very different from what obtains now. In the Bible God's workers are simply God's instruments. We are not told directly of the intellectual power or genius of any of them. We are not told of the great depths in John's mind, or of the fiery energy of Peter, because it was not they or their gifts that did the work, but God working through them. Their light shone before men, not to glorify them, but to glorify their Master. It was not by their power or by their holiness that miracles were wrought, but only through Christ working in them. They did not bring the contribution to which Christ added, but everything in them that really told in His service was from Him. This conception is separated by a wide interval from that which now prevails in the Church.

We hear it said, that if the old teachers and leaders of the Church could be restored, we should see greater things than we now behold; if we had now in the Church the apostles and martyrs of past times, the world would soon be subdued for Christ. That is our mode of thought; but in the Bible it is God that is viewed as the worker. Some of the apostles are nothing more to us than names. They were not meant to be more; for not they did the work, but the Spirit of God working in them. Christ intended to form an enduring kingdom. But in framing it He not only refused to seek the help of earthly governments, but chose as His helpers men so unpromising, that from a merely human point of view they were hindrances. These men were rude fishermen, without intelligence, influence, and wealth. They misunderstand and deny their Master. Yet He chooses them as the material for the most enduring of works. Looking round on them, and knowing them thoroughly, He says with calm certainty, "Fear not, little flock: it is your Father's good pleasure to give you the kingdom."[1]

How is it that when Jesus died, His kingdom spread far more rapidly than when He was living? He surely spake as never man spake; and when His voice was silent, His disciples might well despair of winning a victory which even He had not gained. But they did not despair; and the reason was, that it was not they who spoke, but the Spirit of the Master working in them. They themselves would have deprecated much of the adulation that is paid to their names, and pointed away from themselves to the Master, saying, "Why gaze ye at us, as though by our own power or our own holiness we had done these wonders?"

The apostles, then, while their whole history bears testimony to the brotherliness, the patience, and the tender humanity of Christ, after all are the best witnesses of His power and divinity; for He is not only far above them, but whatever heights they have attained to, are heights to which He has lifted them.

[1] See the able statement of this argument in R. H. Hutton's *Essays*, i. 137.

X
CHRIST'S INTERCOURSE WITH GOD

"He departed into a mountain to pray."

"So closely art thou in God's heart,
    And God so close in thine;
I marvel which is human part,
    And which is thy divine."
                    W. B. PHILPOT.

CHAPTER X

CHRIST'S INTERCOURSE WITH GOD

WE turn from the public life of Christ, and from its aspect to man, to speak of His interior life and His communion with God. In speaking of the devotions of Christ, the main element we must treat is of course His prayerfulness. But before passing to speak of that, we remark on His relation to the synagogue and to the Bible. He was, as we learn, a regular frequenter of the Jewish synagogue. He was, we are told, in His place there, as His custom was. Six days He laboured and did all His work, but the seventh day was the Sabbath of the Lord His God. He might have spent it among the hills round His home, and thus escaped the death-like monotony of the synagogue. But He knew that the best preparation for His teaching was the reverent estimation of the old service. Besides, His own soul was nourished amongst the worshippers. He heard the word of His Father through all the misrepresentations which overlaid it. The prayers might be dull and unaspiring, but there was at least a worshipping and bowing down before the Lord our Maker. So He was there; no more patient, devout, and humble listener than He.

The incident is deeply instructive, as showing the true place of public worship. No wise defender of public worship ever rested his case on the ability of the preacher. Many preachers are men of limited intelligence and feeble emotions, — much inferior in these respects to some among their hearers. The interval, however, to say the least, is not what existed between the teachers at Nazareth and Jesus. Men may read at home sermons far more profound and eloquent than they can hear in church. Still their true place is in the sanctuary; for this is still a custom of Christ's, to be where His people are gathered. Where but two or three are met in His name, He is there in the midst of them.

Further, we have seen already that He was a profound student of the Bible in His early life. During those long years of preparation, His chief companion was His Father's word. He studied Moses, pondered the meaning of the mystery of the Psalms, traced the line of golden testimony through all the prophets to Himself. We remember how well that knowledge served Him in His years of conflict. We remember how, with that sword of the Spirit, He made Satan himself to reel, and taught the sufficiency of Scripture in the worst crises of life. We know how He made his minions to stagger under the same weapon. "Have ye never read," He said in thunder more than once to purblind students of the Bible, who had vainly spent their lives in the study of the letter, seeing nothing of the spirit, — "have ye never read," and confounded and routed them as He had done the Adversary in the wilderness. Even words of that book were made, we know, the foundation of elaborate arguments. But that does not give the whole case. He not only knew the Bible intellectually, and used it as a sharp weapon in attack and defence, He knew it spiritually. He loved it, and trusted it, and sought it in the hour of His agony. It was to Him food during those forty days in which He fasted in the wilderness. Not by bread, but by the word that proceeded out of the mouth of God, did He live then. And so throughout His life the Bible was to Him a fountain of solace and refreshment in the midst of care and conflict. And, as we shall see, when the bitterness of death came, and when that bitterness was bitterest, He fled to the Bible for words of appeal and consolation. "My God! my God! why hast thou forsaken me?" He cried when the darkness was at its worst; and, "Father, into thy hand I commend my spirit," were the words with which His soul approached its Father. He died amid the solemn music of an ancient psalm; and so to Him, in life and in death, the Bible furnished not only weapons for intellectual controversy, but food convenient to nourish and stay the soul.

We come now to speak of His prayerfulness. In one sense, the prayers of Christ formed the truest proof of His manhood.[1] His practice of prayer and His exhortations to it are chiefly recorded in the Gospel of Luke, which is pre-eminently a Gospel of the Son of man. We are told, for example, that Jesus prayed after His baptism; that after He had cleansed the

[1] The boldest transcendental flight of the Talmud, according to Deutsch, is its saying: "*God prays.*"—*Remains*, p. 131.

leper He withdrew into the wilderness and prayed; that the choice of the twelve apostles followed a night of prayer; that when Jesus was alone praying, the disciples came unto Him, and Peter made his great confession; that as He prayed the fashion of His countenance was altered. Again, Luke records that His disciples asked to be taught how to pray; and two parables—that of the loaves and that of the widow—are recorded in Luke to enforce the duty of prayer. Besides, the prayer for the establishing of the faith of Peter, and the prayer for the murderers of Christ, are recorded in the same Gospel. This comes naturally from the writer who traces our Lord's descent to Adam, tells the story of His birth and His childhood, and gives many beautiful touches that teach His true manhood and His tender sympathy.

Prayer is what distinguishes man from other creatures. The creatures below him cannot pray; those above him do not need to pray. The angels, for example, render, without ceasing, ascriptions of praise, which are no doubt prayer in an important sense. One clear thought of prayer is communion with God, having His thoughts and His love dwelling and working in us, living under the conviction that we have been chosen by Him to stand and to work in our lot to the end of the days. But here we speak specially of prayer as request for some needed boon. The manhood of Christ never comes nearer to us than when we remember that He too needed to ask for gifts and for help. We know how His physical nature needed to be supported: how He was weary and thirsty by the well, how He broke down in tears at the tomb, and slept soundly through the storm that almost wrecked the little ship. But we need still more to know that His spirit also was dependent, under submission, and in need; that in communion He was our pattern; that He lived by faith; and that, although His life might be called one long prayer, still He needed, as we do, special seasons of supplication to God. It would not have been wonderful if He had given this, as the angels do, in prayers consisting of mere ascriptions of praise and adoration; but we shall find that we have in the Gospels as real and genuine pleadings for a boon as any man ever offered.

There is the other side of the case. While Jesus Christ was true man He was also true God; and as in other words and deeds of His life we have traced a double side,—true manhood and true Godhead,—not separate, but always together, so in prayer we shall find the same. And we may conveniently arrange our thoughts upon the prayers of Jesus Christ, by considering them,—first, as showing His true manhood; and, secondly, as showing His true divinity.

Looking first at the prayers which show the true humanity of Christ, we take, first, that which He offered before He chose the apostles. His enemies had been seeking to take His life away. He went and chose twelve, as if to multiply His influence and make it indestructible; but before the choice He continued all night in prayer. We can see how large were the issues wrapped up in this selection,—how much, humanly speaking, all the fortune of His kingdom in the world depended upon it; and so, as a preliminary to this solemn act, He prayed all night. In the same way we find Him praying before He revealed to His disciples the suffering that was drawing near. We too may well pray before we make a great choice or speak a decisive word. Were we to pray, the heavenly wisdom granted in answer might save us many a blunder, many a retractation, many an agony. We should be able to walk with sure strength and courage, even by new and difficult roads, if we saw the Wonderful Counsellor before taking the great steps that determine the course and the issue of our lives. In every life, no matter how insignificant it may seem absolutely, there occur circumstances and crises as important relatively as these were to Christ. When these opportunities are misused, and these problems erroneously decided, the errors, for the most part, are irretrievable. To be saved from these errors, we should look up to God after the manner of Christ, and do nothing till an answer has come from the sacred place to our question, "Lord, what wilt thou have me to do?"

Again, we find that Jesus Christ not only prayed before great and decisive acts, but that He prayed after them. He prayed after service as well as before. For example, when He wrought the great miracle of feeding the multitudes, which we have previously referred to as in some respects the miracle that made the deepest impression upon the people, and most undeniably showed His divine power, He went and snatched a brief hour or two of repose, and after that rose early in the morning and engaged in prayer to God. This teaches us much which it is easy but fatal to miss.

When we have done some great work by immense expenditure of force, we are tempted to say our part is done,—we cannot accomplish more. Many a man desires to end and crown his public life amidst the shoutings of applause for some victory or achievement. He would retire to boast of it, and live all the rest of his days upon that proud memory. Better it is to pray,—to pray, if it be God's will, for new strength, for new if humbler efforts, and if that is denied, for blessing on what has been attempted or done. Jesus Christ did not boast, He did not give up, but He recruited Himself for new service by continuing in prayer to God. Another temptation is to pride. We are lifted above the simplicity and humility in which we lived before. Our hearts swell, and we are tempted to think our previous life mean and insignificant. Never are we further from God than when intoxicated by pride. In the pride of their hearts the wicked angels fell, and we may fall too unless we are delivered from their sin. Nothing will avail more effectually to allay and silence our pride than prayer. In communion with our Father our pride is chilled and destroyed. A kindred temptation after great achievements is the temptation to profound depression. When one has done one's utmost, and put forth the whole force of life, one feels completely spent, as if work were over. Men who have preached with power to multitudes of people, have told us of the terrible languor which succeeds a full outburst of the heart. They have told us how they felt as if their life went from them in that supreme effort, and could never be regained. That is natural; and we may learn from Jesus Christ how it is to be met. Let us pray that by prayer and service we may be taught to feel that our well-springs are in God, and that He who strengthened and filled us for that achievement, which we fear we can never repeat, can gird us, if He will, for new and nobler work. The profound truth, after all, is that the greatest thing man can do is to pray. The true climax of his life is not some dazzling public achievement. There is something greater and nobler in the silence of the secret chamber, in wrestling before God for a blessing on the message he has delivered. The preacher is then really higher than he was when he delivered the message. Man experiences his greatest privilege in communion with his God. It is easy to misinterpret the old adage, which says, "To labour is to pray." While it is true in one sense, in another it is false. In a full life there must be both prayer and labour. In a life that is all work, true religion must pine and languish. In a life spent in prayer, without actual service, there is apt to be a luxurious and selfish religion. Christ spent His day in service, but rather than miss prayer He borrowed the hours from sleep, because He knew well that prayer and work must in a true life always go together.

Once more, the Son of man teaches us to pray before and during great agonies. During the great agony of Gethsemane, and before the death of the cross, He prayed more earnestly than any other; yea, He outvied Himself, for His sweat fell upon the ground like great drops of blood, which mingled with the tears of His strong crying. We almost fear that the agony is to be too much for Him, that the flesh is too weak, and that the spirit must shrink from effort.

But He prays, and as the voice of pleading rises, gradually the storm of His spirit is assuaged; strength comes from heaven; and He obtains a victory so complete, that He is borne unmoved through all the trial, carrying Himself with wondrous dignity and patience before His captors and judges, and giving His life a ransom for many.

We travelling onwards can see, not far ahead, great wrenches, and losses, and humblings that we must encounter. The mere brooding over the sorrows that must come to all who live, will not help us to bear them, but we shall be helped if we pray. There are those who feel no cross, and expect none; but the cross will come to all, whether they are the disciples of Christ or not. As the Eastern saying has it, "Every dwelling-place, even if it have been blessed ever so long, at last will become a prey to wind and woe." But those who pray will find that Christ carries the heavy end, and for all that may come, yea, even for the sundering of soul and body in death, we shall be prepared by prayer.

We turn, in the second place, to look at the manifestation of the divinity in prayer. We have seen Him true man, but we do not miss the landmarks of the true God. First of all, in reading the prayers of Jesus Christ, we miss instantly one of the most prominent features of our prayers. In His prayers there is no contrition, no sense of sin, no prayer for pardon. Even in the dire extremity, when there are none to help Him, when refuge fails Him, when no man cares for His soul, when He is forsaken even by His Father, He asks why, well knowing that the reason is not His own sin. In this He contrasts remarkably with His own followers and disciples. They make much of sin; their prayers are largely confession. It seems as if sometimes, when they had confessed their sin until the mouth was opened wide, they did no more but left it to God to fill it. And we find also that the holier they grew, the more unholy they felt themselves to be; the nearer they approached God, the more clearly did they perceive the glory of His holiness, and in that glory every spot, speck, and stain in themselves stood out. We find that the prayers of the Bible are very much made up of confession. It is touching to read in the prayers of our fathers the expressions of their broken-heartedness for "the sins whereby we have made ourselves less than the least of all thy mercies, and provoked thee to embitter all our comforts." But the prayers of Christ, earnest, agonised, tearful as they were, have in them no word of confession. He bore our sins in His own body and in His own soul, yet He Himself had no taint of sin: He was the spotless Son of God. And so in the longest prayer of His we have recorded, the preface is not a confession of sin but an assertion of righteousness: "I have glorified thee on the earth; I have finished the work thou gavest me to do." "Into thy hands," He said, last of all, "I commend my spirit." But He did not say, as we do, "for thou hast redeemed me," because He needed no redemption, being Himself the Redeemer.

Further, it is very striking that though He prayed often for men and before men, He never prayed with men. We rejoice to pray with each other, and He has encouraged us to do so. Exceeding great and precious promises are bound up with the prayer of two or three together. We cannot speak in His name without speaking in His ear; even where but two are gathered together, He will make the third. But He never prayed with any one. He prayed before His disciples, but not with them. He never said along with His disciples, "Our Father," lifting up common petitions for both. He never even said "Our Father" when speaking of Himself and the disciples. He makes the distinction, "Your Father and my Father—your God and my God," as if, even in His closest approaches to them, there was an infinite distance between man and God. He prayed many a time for His disciples, but He never asked their prayers. Their sympathy, indeed, He was thankful for; but though He prayed often that their faith might not fail, He never asked them to plead that His might stand.

Again, when He prayed He received special manifestations of the divine favour. Having referred to these elsewhere, we need not say much of them now. Thus at the Baptism, when He was dedicated to His work, and when the voice of God attested Him as His Son, we are told that He was praying. At the Transfiguration He became clad in raiment like snow; His form was illuminated, and He was transfigured before His disciples. And then, again, God spake to Him. Now it is clear that these manifestations were in a sense lonely and supernatural. We cannot share in them fully, and yet there is a part that we need not miss. At the Transfiguration, when He prayed, the weariness, the wrinkles, the marks of pain went out of His face, and He received His true likeness; and even to men something of the same wonderful light has come and may come. If we want to have the wrinkles wiped out of our face, and be transfigured with the coming glory, and to have the stains of sin washed away, we too must pray. Especially in death, when it is noble and believing, there may be seen something of that smile which was on the face of Stephen when he beheld Christ. There may be even in life that light like an Italian morning on the face. It will come if we pray. He will say to us even, "Thou art my son," and we shall know it to be true in spite of all that makes against it,—in spite of sin, and sorrow, and death. But such manifestations as these received by Christ in answer to His prayers must be held to mark Him out as divine.

Again, the most superficial reader cannot but feel, in perusing especially the intercessory prayer of Christ, that its tone is quite different from any prayer of ours. He makes Himself equal with God. It is probable that the prayer was lifted in the Temple courts. At the Passover the gates of the Temple were opened at midnight. But whether this be so or not, He prays standing upon the steps of the throne. "This is life eternal, that they might know thee the only true God, and Jesus Christ whom thou hast sent." "All mine are thine, and thine are mine, and I am glorified in them." Is that the voice of a man? Does not He speak who counts it no robbery to be equal with God?

Then mark how He prays here. He does not plead as the frail unworthy suppliant, uncertain of the issue of his prayer, but He is as one who has power with God and who prevails. "Father, I will that they also whom thou hast given me may be with me where I am, that they may behold my glory which thou hast given." Praying for Himself, He uses the language of deep submission; but, praying for others, He speaks the tranquil irresistible word we would not dare to use. "My glory," He says, when the glooms of death were thickest,—"the glory which I had with thee before the world was, and will have after the world has been." So we see that, though He was true man, and prayed like us with tears and agonies and cries, nevertheless even in the deepest hour of darkness He was God; and His Godhead shines luminous through all His sorrow, and we know Him to be the eternal Son of God who has become man.

We repeat, then, in closing, that His humanity teaches us to pray as a preliminary before solemn duty, as a rest after service, and as a preparation for great agonies. We are taught His divinity by the entire absence of confession of sin from His prayers, by the loneliness of His prayers, by the wonderful effect they produced, and by His speaking to God in prayer as to His equal.

It is deeply suggestive to reflect that He is still the praying Christ, only now He is the Intercessor. Before Gethsemane He said, "Sit ye here while I go and pray yonder." He says to us now, "Labour, struggle, suffer, pray, while I go and pray yonder." He is praying for us, and by and by He will pray us into heaven. The day will come when it will be His time to say for one, for another, "Father, I will that he whom thou hast given me may be with me where I am, to behold my glory."

XI
CHRIST DEALING WITH INQUIRERS

"I saw all Israel scattered upon the hills, as sheep that have not a shepherd."

"He took the suffering human race,
He read each wound, each weakness clear,
And struck his finger on the place,
And said, *Thou ailest here and here.*"

M. ARNOLD.

CHAPTER XI

CHRIST DEALING WITH INQUIRERS

MUCH of the Gospels is taken up with conversations between Christ and individuals. Teaching so startling and difficult as His, with such an element in it of attraction and hope, naturally drew around Him many who sought to know further what this gospel meant. He on His part was as eager to meet inquirers as they were to seek Him; and we find that He bestowed as much care and pains in expounding the nature of His kingdom to individuals, as He did when He was speaking to great multitudes. The audience, if small, was fit.

Not only so, but we find that He put Himself in the way of individuals. He came to seek souls as well as to save. The shepherd goes after the sheep—after that which is lost. If his track seem erratic, it is because the sheep has wandered first. So it is with Jesus. We seem to see Him seeking, wandering, as it were, aimlessly up and down the land,—now in a crowd, now in solitude, now in a house full of guests, now upon the sea-shore. We find Him looking into the faces of men, calling them from sycamore trees, or by wayside wells; and if we ask why He wandered thus, and why His life-course was not more definite, perhaps the best answer is that He was seeking, and that His course was determined by the track of the sheep. Out of the numerous stories we may select for study the conversation between Christ and the woman of Samaria, and that beween Him and the rich young ruler. One of these issued in salvation, the other in departure from Christ; and the contrast seems to furnish some important teaching as to the upbuilding of the new kingdom.

1. Jesus Christ seeking His sheep must needs go through Samaria. Travelling in the heat of noon, He was thirsty, and sat down by Jacob's Well; but He had nothing to draw with, and the well was deep. The Creator sat by the waters He Himself had created, and looked down into their cool depths in the burden and heat of the noontide. Being weary, He sat thus by the well, making no effort to disguise His weariness,— stretched out in lassitude beneath the burning sun. He is lying thus when the woman comes to Him from a neighbouring village. She was, we know, a woman who had lost her fair name, and this, it may be, brought her forth at a time when others were glad to rest. When He saw her, another thirst awoke in the Saviour. Only sometimes did the body thirst, but the thirsty soul would not let Him rest, and had brought Him here. With the thirst of the body the thirst of the soul rose, and made Him forget His natural thirst, and set Himself to win this lost sister.

To His request for a draught of the cool water He received the reply, "How is it that thou, being a Jew, askest drink of me, who am a woman of Samaria? for the Jews have no dealings with the Samaritans." She did not know that this Jew had dealings with the Samaritans — with all nations and countries. After what fashion He dealt with her we shall see.

First, He wakened in her mind the sense of need. Forgetting His need of water for the body, He spoke of water that should quench thirst for evermore,— of a well that sprang in the soul, and never ceased to yield its sweet abundance. "The water that I shall give him shall be in him a well of water springing up into everlasting life." As yet she understood not His words, but her soul darkly felt their beauty. She thought of her long journeys in the Eastern noon, and of the need in her heart of something that would satisfy; and she prays, "Sir, give me this water, that I thirst not, neither come hither to draw." It was a poor prayer, but it was a beginning. It was with her as it was with the prodigal in the parable, for not love but need drew him home. In that hunger-ridden land he dreamed of plenty, and saw his father's house; but what he saw there was not fulness of love, but fulness of bread. Even the hired servants, whom he had so often ordered about, had bread enough and to spare, so that the very beggars did not depart hungry. That abundance of bread made him rise. "I will go to my father; I will say unto him, Make me as one of thy hired servants"; in other words, "Give me bread and to spare." Bread and to spare was all the heaven which such a soul could in the meantime conceive. It was very little, but it was a beginning. And so, "I perish with hunger," said he, "and I with thirst," said she; and, hungry and thirsty, their souls faint within them, they turned their faces fatherwards and homewards. But the conversation deepens. It was not enough that she should be convinced of her need for salvation; she had to be convinced also of her sin. "Go, call thy husband," He says, "and come hither." The command seemed strangely irrelevant, but He who knows what is in man and woman well knew what He did. The Great Physician of souls shows His skill; He is not only the healer of disease, but its detector. To know what the disease is, is the first and essential step towards curing it, and the step which we often find it hardest to take. He took it now with sovereign inerrancy. He looked at her from head to foot with those clear eyes over which nothing could cast any glamour; He perceived her sin, and He touched its secret place. We grope clumsily for the place of disease, and spread our ointments often where we should not. He, making no mistake, struck her to the heart, pierced her conscience, and brought out all the story of her life.

It was now vain to disguise. She said, "I have no husband," half shrinking and half wishing that He might prove His knowledge and His claims. With a sad irony Jesus replies, "Thou hast said well, I have no husband; and he whom thou hast is not thy husband." We cannot tell now all the wicked and bitter story wrapped up in that,—the story of shame, and crime, and heartlessness that these words covered. Enough to know that they seemed to contain her whole history. "Sir," she said, "I perceive that thou art a prophet." There was no use for further disguise.

Now her heart and life lay bare to His eyes. He was a prophet, and she was a sinner; and there she stood naked and ashamed before Him.

One sin He had told, but all were told with it. "He told me all things that ever I did." Good and evil alike were in that story. There might have been love true and undefiled as well as lawless passion; but whatever there was, He, in telling the one sin, had told it even as He had known it all. How often does it happen that the whole of life is the history of one sin! All that went before has led up to that sin, and all that comes after carries with it the shadow and the pain of that sin; so, when it is dragged into the daylight, all before and after is dragged out with it. When he plucked the sin out of her bosom for her deliverance' sake, it seemed to her as if all her life were shining in the glare of His omniscience. The question which follows has been strangely misunderstood. She confessed Him to be a prophet; and it has been said, to a Samaritan no question could appear more worthy of a prophet's decision than the settlement of the religious centre of the world. But surely one moved as she had been, sought something more vital, more personal? She had come to herself, and, having come to herself, she sought her Father. The sense of need and the sense of sin drove her to seek her God; and "Where," she says, "is He to be found?" "Our fathers," she said, "worshipped in the mountain towering beside us. Must I go to the far Jerusalem to find Him? Can I not find Him on the hill where my fathers found Him?" The Saviour, speaking neither of Gerizim nor Jerusalem, tells her that God is a spirit, and that they that worship Him must worship Him in spirit and in truth.

The words were too deep for her bewildered soul; she would have been lost in them, had it not been that she looked forward to an explainer. "Messias cometh, which is called Christ; when He is come He will tell us all things. He will expound what is now so obscure." The pronoun "He" is emphatic; that teacher would make clear what she could understand from none other. But she was nearer light than she knew; she had not to go to the strange unfriendly city to find Him. She had not to wait for the Messiah. The Word was nigh her—the eternal Word. "I that speak unto thee am He." When He said that to her, they looked the look that is at once an avowal and a covenant. Their eyes met, and their souls met never to part more. She who had come to know her need and her sin, had come to know her Saviour, and knowing Him knew the Father. What follows is full of interest. Upon this came His disciples, who marvelled that He talked with the woman, yet no man said, "What seekest Thou?" or, "Why talkest Thou with her?" He had upon His face that rapture which is faintly figured by the joy of the shepherd finding the sheep, or even by the joy of the earthly father regaining the lost son. He had in His face the joy of the Saviour who has found a lost soul. None dared to speak, until at length, seeing how worn He was, remembering how long it was since He had eaten with them, His disciples humbly implored Him to eat. But He needed not water from the well, or bread from the town. He had meat to eat that they knew not of.

"My meat," said He, "is to do the will of Him that sent me, and to finish His work." And then with glowing eyes He looked forward, and, with one ear of corn in His hand, He saw the harvests that were yet to be,—saw the fields white, and the corn falling before the sickle,—saw the disciples doing the work that He could only begin,—and was glad in the thought that He that sowed and they that reaped would rejoice together. When read sympathetically, nothing in the Gospels is more profound and touching than the insight this gives us into the workings of the Saviour's heart; nothing shows more clearly what was His real delight, and how dear to Him was the purpose of His life. The joy was not transient, for the woman carried the gospel to her countrymen, and for two glad days He sowed and reaped together.

2. The story of the rich young ruler is a complete contrast to that we have now narrated. At first sight it appears a far more promising case than the other. Instead of a Samaritan adulteress, we have a young, beautiful, and, as man speaks, a pure soul. So amiable was he, that although still unredeemed, we are told that Jesus loved him. He was young, and, as has been said, youth itself with health is wealth. "Wealth is in happy heaps that seem exhaustless. Oh for an untried, unstained, unsuspicious heart! might the miser sigh, sitting wearily on his chest of gold. Oh for the eyes that shed the sunshine by which they saw, and that fired only in hate of wrong and love of beauty! Oh for the feet that broke from a walk into a run for very joy! Oh for a back too strong

to bend in servility, and knees not too stiff to kneel in worship!"[1] And besides, he was pure. He had kept all the commandments from his youth up. He had not consciously stooped to evil; and all ignorant though he was of the sin and weakness so soon to be revealed to him, yet after his groping fashion he had chosen the good part, which many might envy him. Many a worn-out debauchee might look at such a young frank face and say:

> " To know good is to love it;
> And the honour that I covet
> Is the pride of your pure youth."

Besides, he was rich, and riches tend to repress and chill the soul. It was something that he was what he was, in spite of all his riches; that he had kept from drinking the cup of pleasure; and that in his high place he had loved righteousness more. We need not shrink from frankly allowing these things, for Jesus beholding him loved him.

Besides, there was something winning in his mode of approach. In the case of the Samaritan woman, Christ had to pierce through the dull crust of sin and worldliness that lay round her heart; He had to waken the desire He was afterwards to satisfy. It was not so here, for he came running, as if with an earnest desire,—as if afraid his enthusiasm would cool before he gained the gift. He came reverently, for he knelt and said, "Good Master." He went straight to the heart of the question: "What shall I do that I may inherit eternal life?" Look at the two pictures,

[1] T. T. Lynch.

Christ dealing with Inquirers

and say whether the Lord will not deal more gently with the rich young ruler than with the woman of Samaria.

So we say in our ignorance, looking at the two, and seeing on the one no mark of disease, and on the other disease in all its foulness. But Jesus looks with the eyes that cannot be deceived, and immediately takes hold of the young man's question, and asks him what it means. "Good Master!" what does that mean? It is a graceful epithet. Is it mere politeness? is it the mere effervescence of an amiable nature? or do you know all that is meant by saying "Good Master"? Christian apologists are blamed sometimes for putting the dilemma, that Christ is either God or He is not good. They are told that such a style of argument will either kill or cure. But they may plead great authority, for that is what Christ Himself does. He pulls him up sharply, not because he was irreverent, but because he was superficial. "There is none good but one; that is God. If I am good, I am God; and there is no medium." He goes on: "If thou wilt enter into life, keep the commandments." The answer came with a shock of disappointment. The rich young ruler wanted to do something more,—something new and great,—when he was told to pace the old round. "Keep the commandments!" Why, he had given them a lifelong obedience! "Keep the commandments!" Had this new teacher nothing more to say to him? He had: "Go and sell all that thou hast, and give to the poor; and come, take up thy cross and follow me." He thought he had kept all the commandments, but here was one commandment interpreted, and he falls. The Lord goes into the chamber of his heart, and finds seated there the horrid idol Mammon. It was too much: the young man made the great refusal—he turned away.

What was the meaning of such a strange demand? It cannot be implied that all who trust in Christ need to part with their possessions. We must fall back upon Christ's certain knowledge of man. He saw into the depths of that soul, and perceived that its ultimate rest was riches; and as salvation must be the rest of the soul on Christ, that prop had to be taken away at whatever cost. It was not that he was so grossly ignorant as to think that riches would purchase eternal life; nor was he so vulgar as to boast of his riches offensively. The soul was of finer fibre than that, else Jesus would not have loved it. But his riches were, after all, the main element of his happiness. There were many things probably between his happiness and its foundation,—so many things, that he did not know that the real foundation was money. Still, so it was; and if the riches had been taken away, the whole content and happiness of his life, his very amiability, would have vanished with them. It was not that he clutched his wealth, not that he was niggardly, but his life was his wealth—it was his rest; and if he had been a completely beggared man, he could not have stood free and clear in God's world; or, to put it more plainly, the loss of his means would have killed him, as it has killed many a one.

We need to make a very short and sharp reckoning with whatever comes between us and our trust in Christ. If we will not, He will, and friend and lover will be put far from us, and the edifice of our fortune shattered, that we may lean upon Christ alone. The test was a very sharp one, but nothing less would do; and so he said, "I cannot take up my cross, if I must lay down my gold. I cannot go up to Jerusalem, if I have to go up to die." So then he went away sorrowful, for he had great possessions. Whether he returned we cannot tell. He might,—we may hope he did,—because he did not leave carelessly, and because he was loved by Christ. "O man whom Jesus loved, didst thou ever love Him in return? and as thou once camest glad and wentest away grieved, didst thou ever come grieved and go away glad? Did thy blossom bear no fruit?" Was he not saved if so as by fire? We know not; but even if he was, he had missed a great opportunity—an opportunity which never could return. He went away sorrowful. And he left behind him a sorrowful Christ. Else why the melancholy refrain, "How hardly shall they that have riches enter the kingdom of God! It is easier for a camel to pass through the eye of a needle, than for a rich man to enter the kingdom of God." How wistfully He gazed after him departing from life and light. We speak and think much of the sorrow of the disappointed inquirer, but what of the sorrow of the rejected Master? There is no sorrow like that sorrow. The same pang shot through Him as made Him weep over unsheltered and doomed Jerusalem, that so often might have been gathered had He but had His will.

A few lessons may be drawn from the contrast. There is first the old lesson, needing ever to be repeated, of the preciousness of one soul. The greatest words of Christ were spoken to one soul, the greatest joy ministered by one. "There is joy in the presence of the angels over one." "Where two or three are gathered in my name, there am I in the midst of them." One soul is an end worthy of all the effort of Deity, and therefore worthy of all ours. Many a heart has been made sad, that God has not made sad, by refusing to be satisfied with what delighted the Saviour. To save even one soul is honour enough to crown a lifetime. Out of one soul's salvation issues of inconceivable magnitude may flow. To convert one may be to convert a continent; but whether or not we see this—whether or not we can cipher it out correctly—we may be sure that one soul in itself is an end for which we may strive with all our power, and over which we may rejoice with all our heart.

Again, we mark that Christ did not try to gain those who might profit His cause in a worldly sense. He never bought adherents by unworthy means. We can easily see that in some ways the adherence of the rich young ruler might be profitable, while the conversion of the Samaritan woman might rather discredit Him than otherwise. His disciples marvelled that He talked with the woman, and they marvelled still more that He sent the rich young ruler away. "Who then," they said, "can be saved?" But He never bought adherents by worldly means, and never sought to gather into His kingdom those who were not with it in heart. His success was not to be judged by numbers. It is pleasant to see great numbers gathering round the standard, but quality is more than quantity. Those who gather themselves around Christ must be strong men who have trusted Him, who have entered by the strait gate, and who have left behind them all other grounds of trust. The gate was not broad enough to admit the rich young ruler with his burden of wealth; there was room only for the soul, and so he was left outside. Jesus Christ looked forward to the time when men should say, "Lord, Lord," and enter in this way the portals of the Church visible, but into the Church invisible none could pass save those who had His spirit.

We are taught also that sin does not shut the door, and that morality does not open it. The Samaritan woman entered before the rich young ruler; publicans and harlots entered before Pharisees. Why? Because they were forlorn, because they had nothing else to lean on, and therefore leant hard on Christ. The rich young ruler had respectability and riches. He was not sure if they were able to sustain him, and yet he would not take the risk of quitting them for Christ, and so he is shut out. He went away sorrowful, for he had great possessions. The woman of Samaria entered that door which is open to the wretched and the guilty, for the Son of man is come to seek and to save that which was lost,

XII
CHRIST'S REPLIES TO HIS ENEMIES

"Out of his mouth went a sharp two-edged sword."

"When the pitcher falls on the stone, woe to the pitcher; when the stone falls on the pitcher, woe to the pitcher; whatever befalls, woe to the pitcher."—THE TALMUD.

CHAPTER XII

CHRIST'S REPLIES TO HIS ENEMIES

WE cannot fully estimate Christ, unless we see Him as He was when He was put upon His defence. How did He meet His enemies? The subtlest intellects in the country opposed Him—who outwardly was nothing more than a poor peasant, who had never learned. We know how He could speak when He had time and opportunity to prepare Himself. How does He answer when He is attacked suddenly?

On one occasion He was assailed in succession by different classes of His enemies. First of all, the elders and chief priests asked Him by what authority He did His works. They hoped to entangle Him, believing that in whatever way He answered He would find Himself in a dilemma. He replied by putting another question, "The baptism of John, was it from heaven or of men?" They found themselves puzzled now, for if they admitted the baptism to be from heaven, then they would acknowledge Christ's claims; and if they denied its heavenly origin, they would find themselves in collision with the people, who reverenced John as a prophet. They took refuge in a cowardly silence: "We cannot tell." Then said He, "Neither tell I you by what authority I do these things." At first sight it seems strange that He should fail to give a clear response to any question about His authority. These men were the appointed rulers of the people, and, apparently, in the strict line of duty in making such an inquiry. And, besides, there is something that at least resembles evasion in the reply—an apparent want of openness and candour. Any difficulty of that sort in the sayings of Christ is well worth examining, for it always covers a large principle, just as precious metal is found in the hardest rocks. The answer was what it was because the question was dishonest. He tears away the veil from the question, and makes them see what it really was. He shows them that they knew, or might know, that the question had been put dishonestly, and therefore did not deserve a reply. Putting the question in that spirit, they could have no answer. There are certain attitudes of mind which shut the mouth of Christ, and there are difficulties which, professing to be intellectual, are in reality moral. This was one of them. For, first of all, their minds were already made up. They had come to the fixed conclusion that Christ was not from heaven; and though they were putting questions, they never meant to believe the answer, if it did not square with their preconceived notions. And so it is in vain for any one to investigate Christianity with a foregone conclusion. Many a one begins the search into the claims of religious truth fully resolved in his own mind that he never will become an old-fashioned Christian; and to such a one the mouth of Christ is shut. They never intended to believe in Him and do His commandments. They had habits and ways of life which allegiance to

Him would rudely break up; but such an allegiance it never entered their minds to render. So many a one begins to investigate Christianity while his life is ruled by habits directly contrary to Christianity, and it needs no prophet to foretell that such an investigation will lead to no result.

These men, besides, could have no answer, because they had neglected the partial answer already received. Light had been given to them, and they had refused that light. "To him that hath shall be given," is as true of Christian light as of anything else. All have a little light to begin with, and that light, if followed, will brighten and at last illuminate the soul. Christ is the true Light, that lighteth every man that cometh into the world. The range of His beams is wide, and any one who will choose a beam and follow the track of light, will find himself at last in the central radiance to which all paths converge. They could not tell. But if they had not willingly closed their eyes they could have told, and if they had not been cowards they would have told. And because they had neglected and rejected the light they had, Christ refuses to give them another gleam. He will not give that which is holy to dogs, neither will He cast pearls before swine.

And, besides, He was silent to these men because they were mere intellectual inquirers. The very last thought that entered their minds was, that they had need of Christ. They came to Him to bandy words, with no thought that, as guilty sinners, they needed His love and pardon. To come to Christ as a clever lawyer comes to browbeat a witness, is to come in vain. There must be the sense of want, otherwise He will refuse to speak to us, and in His very refusal silence and confound us.

Not deterred by the failure of these questioners, came the Pharisees and the Herodians. Of the Herodians we know nothing more than can be inferred from the name, which shows that they were favourable to the ascendancy of Herod and his family. The question they put was, "Is it lawful to give tribute to Cæsar, or not?" and, so far as appearances went, this question also was a perfectly fair one. It was a practical one, and to the Herodian there might be a question between his loyalty to Herod and the demands of a foreign ruler. To the Pharisee it might be a matter of conscience. Cæsar, the arch-enemy of Israel,—his throne on the Babylon of seven hills, his heel on the neck of the covenant people of God, his eagle hovering over the Temple area,—this profane tyrant, was he to be acknowledged by the children of Abraham, Isaac, and Jacob? The question seemed sincere, but was not in reality so. The two had banded themselves together in order to destroy Jesus, this hatred of Him being the one thing they had in common. He had called Herod a fox, and held up the Scribes and Pharisees as a scorn and byword, and they seek to flatter His pride and destroy Him. If He says "Yes," He will forfeit His reputation for courage and His last opportunity of being a popular leader. If He says "No," the Roman authorities will immediately seize and destroy Him.

He makes no direct reply, but asks for a penny—a denarius, the common silver coin of the day, with the stern, cruel, inscrutable face of Tiberius stamped upon it;—"Render unto Cæsar the things that are Cæsar's." The stamp is a mark of ownership; it tells of a fixed Government which rules over their life, and to which its dues must be paid. Our Lord declares not the divine right of Tiberius, but the divine right of law and order. Not content with this, He adds the significant lesson and rebuke, "Render unto God the things that are God's." That is, "Do not be satisfied with doing your duty in the smaller matters,—with cleansing the outside of the cup,—but rise higher, and remember that, as the image of Cæsar is stamped upon that coin, so is the image of God upon you." They were God's coins, issued from Him to return to Him, owing to Him the tribute of themselves. The question they were discussing was of infinitely little importance as compared with the question that they were ignoring. It is the disease of humanity to escape from the real problem which ought to engage the soul, to one which beside it is but frivolous. "Render unto God the things that are God's." The lines upon the coin are blurred, but still the face of God is there, and you are not your own.

Thirdly, once more He was assailed, this time by the Sadducees, who had got up a case which they imagined would puzzle Him. "A woman," they said, "had been married to seven brothers: whose wife should she be in the resurrection?" An imaginary case in all probability, and much credit would the deviser of it take to himself. But how utterly they were defeated! He showed them, as He showed all objectors, that they were *fundamentally* wrong. "In the resurrection they neither marry nor are given in marriage, but are as the angels of God in heaven." And He profoundly argued from the fact that God called Himself the God of Abraham, Isaac, and Jacob, that these departed fathers were still living unto Him. Not declaring a new truth, He showed them what treasures, unknown to them as yet, were to be found in the old revelation.

A lawyer, who might have learned wisdom from all these defeats, now crosses swords with Him, saying, perhaps within himself, "These people have failed because they have not studied the law; they do not know the plans of cross-examination as I do. But I will undertake Him and silence Him." So he puts the question, "Which is the great commandment of the law?" and is silenced by the voice which thunders out, "'Thou shalt love the Lord thy God with all thy heart, and with all thy mind, and with all thy soul, and with all thy strength, that is the first commandment of the law; and the second is like unto it, Thou shalt love thy neighbour as thyself.'" It was enough for the lawyer.

The whole case is not exhibited by the stories of His retorts. Some of the deepest of His sayings were brought forth by enemies. When the Pharisees and Scribes murmured, "This man receiveth sinners, and eateth with them," He told the parables of the sheep that was lost, of the silver piece, and of the prodigal son. It was when a certain lawyer stood up and tempted Him that He spoke the parable of the Good Samaritan, which, next to that of the prodigal son, has been dear to the heart of the world. It was in answer to Simon's suspicion that He told of the creditor who frankly forgave both his debtors.

These instances might be added to. What do they show? They show that the more Christ's mind is drawn out, the richer it is. He is never so great as when He speaks without premeditation in reply to His enemies. Remember who they were and who He was. They were the wise men of the nation, skilled from their childhood in all manner of word-fencing. He was but a poor carpenter, who had just left the bench, who had never learned. What makes Him such an antagonist? Whence has He that wisdom? Why is it that He is never worsted? Why is it that these conflicts always end in the humiliation of His enemies? that He makes the wrath of man to praise Him, and the heathen to sound His trumpet? Is not the man who can do these wonders God with us?

So it has been since He spoke. Attacks on the Christian religion have brought forth replies which have been the fullest exposition of Christian truth. We owe more to the enemy than to the friend. The enemies who attack Him are, in spite of themselves, made to swell the host of His friends. The devil's assaults on the saints have issued in the most pathetic and devotional utterances of the human mind. The Church has been at her greatest when led to prison and to judgment. The blood of the martyrs has been the seed of the Church.

XIII

CHRIST'S TOIL FOR MEN

"I must work the works of Him that sent me, while it is day: the night cometh, when no man can work."

"This life of mine
Must be lived out, and a grave thoroughly earned."
ROBERT BROWNING.

CHAPTER XIII

CHRIST'S TOIL FOR MEN

WE aim in this chapter at giving an idea of the way in which the days of Christ's ministry were spent. Before speaking of His work, something has to be said of His endurance. His sufferings in one sense were solitary and unique, but He had His share also of those pains which every great and noble life has to pass under. He was the enduring Christ, not only in the deep mystery of His atonement when He drank the bitterness of our punishment, not only in the trial agony which He endured as our representative, but in the lifelong pain of His days. He lived surrounded by an atmosphere of calumny and rejection. He was misunderstood by those who were closest to Him in ties of blood. For the gospel's sake He had to break through the bonds which had been confirmed through thirty years of His life. He had to endure the misunderstandings even of His own disciples who were nearest to Him, and to whom He showed most of His heart. And, besides, He lived under the fierce, fiery, watchful hatred of the Pharisees. There is no hatred like the hatred of religionists who fear that their system is to be overthrown, and that hatred He knew to the full. He was dogged by keen and critical malignity. Every action was misinterpreted, every word twisted. Men sought in all things to find materials for accusing Him. This hatred pained Him, as it would pain any—nay, it pained Him more keenly than it could pain us, because of His absolute sinlessness. He felt such a requital, because there was nothing within Him which declared it to be even in a remote degree just. We who indistinctly know our imperfections have the feeling that criticisms passed upon us, if not deserved in one point, are deserved in others. He had no such alleviation. Besides, since He loved all and despised none, every harsh judgment wounded Him. And further, His pain was intense, because He saw that men in thus treating Him were kicking against the goads to their own ruin. When men reject their fellow-men, they for the most part know that the worst suffering will be that of the rejected. Christ knew that the loss and the ruin would be to those who so tried Him, and this consciousness, instead of lessening his pain, made it keener.

Yet He endured the contradiction of sinners against Himself. The word implies more than stoical patience, it signifies an unalterable tenacity of purpose. He abode in His place, saw the plain path, and pursued it in spite of all opposition. This persistence of Christ in His course, the exceeding tenacity with which He pursued His point, is often missed by us, because His purpose never drooped. Had He faltered sometimes, as all men do, and knit Himself up after a temporary swerving, we should have appreciated much more easily the thorough and perfect determination of His life. But the fact that the motive always prevailed makes it more difficult for us to perceive it. And, besides, the exceeding gentleness with which this resolution was as it were sheathed, conceals it from us. A velvet glove is over the iron hand, but it is an iron hand. He endured the contradiction of sinners against Himself. In spite of all the criticisms, all the hatred, all the opposition, He never turned back. He kept His way stedfastly on to the very end.

But besides endurance there was work. His days were full of labour, and in all the labour there was profit. The record of one day from the early part of His ministry will best show the nature of His life. That day He spent in His own city Capernaum, where He had returned from the other side of the Lake of Gennesaret. Capernaum, then a busy thriving town, situated on a pile of rocks overlooking the sea, was for some time His home. In the morning the neighbours came to welcome Him back. There would be in the house, as in other Jewish homes of the same class, a large upper chamber for prayer and social gatherings, and the people flocked in there. While they were with Him, He was interrupted in a singular fashion. A man, whose career of vice had been cut short by paralysis, and who was now apparently approaching his end,—for it is difficult otherwise to explain the manner of his introduction,—was suddenly let down through the roof and laid at His feet. Whatever sins the man had been guilty of, he had at least four good friends left. And these kind-hearted men, in the eagerness of their friendship, had adopted the bold and daring plan of breaking the roof, and putting their poor friend thus down at the feet of Jesus. The man seems to have had less hope than they, for Jesus, looking kindly down on him as he gazed up into His face, answered his unspoken thoughts with the words, "Be of good courage, my child, thy sins are forgiven thee." Some of the venerable doctors in the room had come to test the claims of Jesus, and Jesus first makes the claim of power to forgive sins. They think within themselves that He blasphemes, because none can forgive sins but God. And He answers their unspoken thought by giving a proof of His claim,—confirming the word by action, and triumphantly healing the man. While they were thinking it is easy to say, "Thy sins be forgiven thee," He shows them that He can not only speak but act. Shortly after, He went out with a multitude following Him, and at the receipt of custom He sees a man, Levi. This man had deeply degraded himself in the eyes of his fellow-countrymen by taking service with the Romans. He had to receive the dues of the boats that came into the little port, and the taxes of the caravans that entered the town. It must have been a great grief to his friends to see him where he was, for no true Jew would have taken such work. He had been scourged out of the synagogue, and cut off from his own people, and there he was day by day among his relatives, but not of them. The class of men to which he belonged was execrated by his countrymen, and doubtless there was an honest family in that town to whom he was a constant grief. Jesus cast His eyes upon him and said, "Follow me." And the man rose and followed Him. He left his old life, received a new name,—

the gift of God,—and became a disciple, an apostle of Jesus Christ. This call would make a great sensation—and we find that it did—amongst those of Matthew's own class, as well as others. It showed how utterly indifferent Christ was to worldly considerations in the choice of His disciples. To elect a man who had been a publican would be a stumbling-block to many, but Christ did not follow the maxims of so-called prudence. He called Matthew, and then went out and taught. What He said we cannot tell. The lost words of Christ, what desires, what speculations there have been about these! Science has given us many things back, and we still may gaze on the scenes where the words were spoken. But these lost words of Christ, will they ever be restored? We shall find some of them, doubtless, in heaven, woven into the grateful songs of praise raised by those whom they won.

He taught—how long we do not know, but in the evening we find Him sitting at Matthew's table with a great company of publicans and sinners. Matthew showed his insight into the heart of Christ by asking those publicans and sinners, knowing that their company would be welcome; and he showed his love for his old associates by giving, and they their good feeling for him by accepting, this invitation. He took them to his house, which must have been large and handsome to receive so great a company, and there Jesus must have enjoyed some of His purest draughts of happiness. The Pharisees came in to criticise. Debate commenced, and we have some of the conversation that passed at the table. The question was put, why the disciples did not fast as the disciples of John had done, and Jesus replies in some of His profoundest and most genial words. His kingdom, He explained, was one of joy, and He was yet with His disciples. The time was coming when He would be taken from them, and it would be time enough for them to fast. In the meantime they were to be glad, for His preaching was good news. He illustrated this by the parable of the children of the bride-chamber, who do not mourn, but the reverse, when the bridegroom is with them; and by the parable of the old and new cloth, and the bottles and the wine. Old cloth should not be sewed on to new; old wine should not be put in new bottles. The law of seemliness and congruity should be observed, and yet He says there is something to be said for those who prefer the old, for the old is mild. The mood of Christ at this supper seems to have been exceedingly bright and cheerful. He was where He loved best to be. The Physician was amongst the sick, and He felt Himself at home.

While they were sitting, there suddenly burst in the ruler of the synagogue, Jairus. He was the chief man of the place, and it was strange that he was seen in such a house, for he very probably had scourged Matthew out of the synagogue with forty stripes save one. But he had good reason. His little daughter—a term of endearment, for the girl was twelve, and that age means womanhood in the East—is at the point of death. Jesus went with him down the darkling street, but as they were going along they were stopped by a woman who had an issue of blood. Twelve years had she suffered from it—as long a time as Jairus' daughter had lived. She had spent all her living and was nothing the better, but rather the worse. The disease was one which warranted divorce, and made her unclean. She touched the hem of the Healer's garment with a trembling finger, and virtue went out of Him. He turned round, asked who touched Him, had her brought forward to confess her story, and sent her away with the words: "Thy faith hath saved thee; go in peace." Jairus must have been impatient while this delay took place, knowing all the time that his daughter's life was passing. And when they came to the door there was the tumult of the mourners, which showed that she was gone. But said Jesus, "She is not dead, but sleepeth." He entered the room, took her by the hand, restored her to life and to her parents, and with benignant composure and tenderness commanded that something should be given her to eat.

Surely this was a crowded day; but, as if it were not enough, two blind men cried, "Thou Son of David, have mercy upon us." They followed Him with their cries, but He gave no heed, until at length they cried, "Lord, have mercy upon us." The use of that word, which was not applied even to the emperor, showed great faith, and Jesus saw that they were now fit to receive an answer. He gave it: "According to your faith be it unto you," and they received their sight. Even this is not enough; for when He comes home He is met by a man possessed with a devil. The Evil One became incarnate when the Holy One did, and now they meet. The result is not doubtful. Jesus turns to the man with the calmness of conscious strength, and commands the devil to come out of him. The commandment is instantly obeyed, and the dumb man begins to speak.[1]

Such is a day of the life of Christ, and of the same complexion are all the rest. We find that His toil was prolonged to the point of physical exhaustion. We find that He put aside His own bodily wants for the relief of others. We find that with wonderful and uncomplaining patience He bore the requests, and appeals, and interruptions which were constantly occurring in His life. He made haste to do His work. Looking at the face of the dial, He saw the hours passing, and said, "I must work the works of Him that sent me, while it is day: the night cometh, when no man can work." Is it any marvel that His life was as a fire that burned fiercely? Unsparing toil, continuous passion, habitual emotion, wear the life away.

His was an eminently active life, but its most prominent feature was neither activity nor contemplation, but the way in which activity and contemplation were combined. While He was upon earth, engaged in rude hard work, and enduring pain, He was always surrounded by the presence of God. The ever thronging cares of His ministry never separated Him a moment from the Father. With us the deeply religious spirit is often unable to cope with the disturbing realities of life, and the practical spirit tends

---

[1] I have followed closely the bright and graphic narrative of Mr. S. Cox in *A Day with Christ*. But I have not been able to accept Mr. Cox's attempt to prove that Matthew was Christ's cousin. See Meyer on John xix. 25.

to become hard and poor from want of meditation and prayer. The two are joined here in absolute completeness. Never was there any life more full of tireless activity; never was there any that drank more continuously at the well-springs. None ever bore a greater part in all the activities of life than He; and yet He was the Son of man which is in heaven, and we cannot think of Him as without the celestial background.

XIV
THE TRANSFIGURATION OF CHRIST

"We received from God the Father honour and glory."

"Few the homages and small
That the guilty earth at all
Was permitted to accord
To her King and hidden Lord.
Dear to us for this account
Is the glory of the Mount,
When bright beams of light did spring
Thro' the sackcloth covering.
Rays of glory found their way
Thro' the garment of decay,
With which, as with a cloak, He had
His divinest splendour clad."

R. C. TRENCH.

CHAPTER XIV

THE TRANSFIGURATION OF CHRIST

THERE may be said to be three summits in our Lord's life—the Temptation, the Transfiguration, and the Agony in the Garden. Of these we may perhaps call the Transfiguration the summit level and division. It was the one open manifestation of Godhead. Before, Jesus had been manifested as God only in words and acts; here, He takes on the appearance proper to Divinity. Up to the Transfiguration the faith of the disciples grew until it culminated in the great confession of Simon Peter: "Thou art the Christ, the Son of the living God." And up to the Transfiguration the hostility of His enemies steadily advanced. Before the Transfiguration, miracles were numerous; after the Transfiguration, few, and these few in special circumstances. Before the Transfiguration there had been free and frequent speech in public; after the Transfiguration He talked mainly with His own disciples. It seemed as if all whom words and miracles could move had already been drawn to Him, and so from the summit of the Transfiguration hill He descended quietly into the darkness of death that lay before Him in the valley.

The note of time given in connection with the

Transfiguration is extremely significant. It was eight days after the revelation made to the disciples of the approaching death at Jerusalem. This helps us to understand the bearings of the scene on Christ and on His disciples. Of the two, perhaps the significance of the Transfiguration is more immediately connected with the Lord Himself. In the first place, it was for Him a foretaste of the glory that was to follow. As He stood there on the hill-top, arrayed in that garment of light which scattered the darkness, He was clothed in the apparel proper to Deity, for the raiment of God is light. But the light around Him was more than raiment—it was more than a robe put on from the outside. It was an emanation from the fountain of light within. These were rays that streamed forth from His own nature: and herein is the difference between the Lord and such of His followers as have looked to Him and been lightened. The face of Moses shone, though he was all unconscious of the radiance; and we read of the dying Stephen that his face was as the face of an angel—bright, calm, and pure. But in both these cases the light was derived, and the servants merely reflected the glory that streamed upon them from the face of their Master. Not so with Christ, who Himself was the Light of the world. He was not merely one who bore the light in His hand—He, the Light Himself, rayed out into splendour, upon the full blaze of which we may not look.

Were we to forget this, we might say that the glory of Christ in the Transfiguration was the glory of His soul; not external glory, but the glory of feeling and of will. There was the glory of His self-devotion, of His utter surrender of Himself for the needy world, and there was also the glory of His resolved will, which made Him set His face as a flint to go to Jerusalem, in spite of all that was to meet Him. Without disregarding these, it is safe to conclude that the main element of the glory was the revelation of that Godhead which had been and was to be, for a time, so darkly obscured.

Again, the Transfiguration gave Christ the assurance of the sympathy of heaven in the work that was dearest to His heart. Moses and Elias appeared and talked with Him about the decease He should accomplish at Jerusalem. His great work was to die, and one of the chief sources of His sorrow must have been the want of sympathy from men with that which was dearest to Him. For long, except in veiled allusions, He was not able to speak of His death at all. When at last the tide of feeling burst its barriers, and He opened all His heart, and told His disciples that He must suffer many things, and be killed, and be raised again the third day, even Peter, who had just risen to the height of his great confession, fell, and said: "Be it far from thee, Lord; this shall not be unto thee." He who a few moments before had been called the Rock was rebuked as Satan. Since He could not speak even to His own disciples of His great death, how welcome it must have been for Him to commune with Moses and Elias, who could speak of it with the calm wisdom and satisfying sympathy of heaven! They spoke of the decease which He should accomplish at Jerusalem. The word decease means departure, and so the harshness of death is veiled and chastened in their speech. For what was His death after all? It was a departure, which He should accomplish from the Jerusalem which murdered the prophets and stoned them that were sent unto her, to the Jerusalem which is above, the Mother of the Holy. They two had an easy departure. Moses died, according to the beautiful legend of the Rabbis, by the kiss of the mouth of God. He died in the fulness of his strength, with his eye undimmed and his natural force unabated, while Elijah was carried by a chariot of fire to the courts above. Christ's death was to be more glorious than the departure of these, and it was not so hard as it might seem. It was an exodus He should accomplish at Jerusalem.

If they comforted Him, might not He have said something to comfort them? Though their end had been easy, their life had been hard. Moses died without entering the Promised Land, Elijah ascended without seeing the full triumph of God's cause. Would not the Saviour show them how their work— the work of the lawgiver and the work of the prophet — was taken up and fulfilled in His own life? He would show them how their labour, the issues of which they had not fully understood, was a preparation for, and indeed a necessary preliminary to, His work. For the glory of the work of Christ does not efface and absorb the work of the servants —it only brightens and explains it. He would help them, they would help Him, as they talked together of the great sacrifice that was to be rendered so soon.

We know from other parts of the gospel what solace our Lord found in the sympathy of heaven. Though Pharisees might frown and jeer when sinners were saved, there were mirth and music in the presence of the angels of God. Here He was not ministered to by angels. Those who spoke to Him knew more than angels could of His sorrow in His work, and of the meaning of death. Still it is the sympathy of heaven that is here given as a cordial to help Him on.

Besides, He heard the voice of the Father, "This is my beloved Son, in whom I am well pleased." We can never understand how the approval of the Father gladdened and uplifted the wearied soul of Christ, and so we must leave it, remarking only how much it must have been to Him when it was three times repeated in the great turning-points of His life. There is no need to dwell on the view of Christ's death implied in all this. This death is not a yielding to the malice of men, but the fulfilment of the eternal purpose of God.

We now turn to the bearings of the Transfiguration upon the disciples. They learned, first of all, that the words of Christ about His crucifixion and death were altogether true. The staggering revelation which they understood so little, and forgot so soon, was emphasised by the authoritative word from heaven, "Hear ye Him." That commandment we need just as they needed it. In the presence of the cross of Christ, after all the explanation we can give, there remains much which is a deep mystery.

Before the darkness we stand speechless. We cannot reason; we cannot understand; we must believe. He is the beloved Son. We hear Him, believing that the mysteries we in vain desire to look into shall at last be unfolded by Himself. Still further, the disciples were prepared by special revelation for the great trial that was to come. They had the Lord's divinity manifested before their eyes, and this vision was to remain, and did remain in some measure, before them when the shadows and sorrows of death encompassed Him around. So, when things grow darker with us and yet darker, we are, for the most part, prepared by some special provision of timely grace bestowed before, lest we should faint in the greatness of our way. So much so that Christians have learned, after a wonderful manifestation of divine love, to expect some trial in the darkness of which that manifestation would be the rest and refuge of the soul. Yet again, we see here Christ's mission confirmed by the representatives of preceding dispensations. These ancient princes—elect of the elect—represented the one the law and the other the prophets. The law and the prophets bore their witness, and set their seal to the atoning work of Christ. He was to be crucified for setting aside the law, and for falsely assuming to be the Messiah; and yet here we have Moses and Elias talking and sympathising with Him, as if Moses said, "My law has not been destroyed but fulfilled"; and Elias, "Those wonders which we darkly foretold have been fulfilled in Jesus the Son of God."

But still further, the disciples needed to learn that

Christ's true glory was in suffering. His glory was full of grace. They saw nothing in the cross but shame and defeat. This vision was to teach them that His cross was His throne. It seemed to them that He had completely lost His glory when He went to die. They had to be taught the victory of defeat —the glory and the gain of loss; for the outer trappings in which they supposed the glory to lie were mere accessories, and when they were given up of His own free will, the burning heart of the glory only blazed the brighter. He never was so glorious as He was in His bending love and His stooping pity. God forbid that we should glory, save in the cross of the Lord Jesus Christ.

Still further, they needed to learn the supremacy of Christ. Peter says, "Let us make here three tabernacles—one for thee, one for Moses, and one for Elias." He did not realise the unapproachable greatness of Christ. He would have put them all on the same level. But he is rebuked, when Moses and Elias vanished from the hill, and when to their eyes lifted up in wonder there appears Jesus only. Jesus was left alone. Moses and Elias vanished, as all preparatory dispensations vanish; as, indeed, all things and all men will ultimately vanish save Himself. They shall perish, but Thou remainest. From dying eyes all will pass save Jesus only.

The modern mind has in some measure learned one of these great lessons. The glory of self-devotion that lighted up the hill, and scattered the shadows and glooms of death, has never been more extolled than it is now by those who have failed to see the glory of the cross of Christ. But it may be found that all self-sacrifice that is persistent and really helpful to the race, must ultimately derive its force from the self-sacrifice on Calvary. There can be no true enthusiasm of humanity without faith in a personal God and Father, and this Father is given to us in the cross of Christ. Without this faith a man may attempt to lessen the sum of human misery; but the effort will soon collapse. For if there be not a good Lord on our side, is it not like an attempt to empty the sea, and, what is more, an attempt to empty it without proving that what we are doing is the best fitted to attain the object? Besides, where without the cross is the motive for self-sacrifice? The Christian spirit is the heroic spirit, willing to give itself. But the reasons must be worthy and noble. The Christian spirit is shown not simply in giving up this world, or accepting pain and want, but in doing this, if it must be done, *for that for which it is worth a man's while to do it*— for something of corresponding greatness, though unseen; for work, for faith, for duty, for the good of others, for a higher life.[1] This view can be beheld only from the cross. How soon was Christ called upon to use the strength He had received! He had been in heaven for these few hours, all night on the hill with Moses and Elias. He must have felt as if the New Jerusalem had descended from heaven from God. It was good for Him to be there, and His soul was doubtless strung into an ecstasy of high rapture. But round the hill there rolled darkly the

[1] See the masterly remarks of Church : *Sermons*, p. 68.

The Transfiguration of Christ

sea of sin and sorrow, and it was not long before He heard its moaning. Familiar though it was in His present mood, it stung Him with a sudden pain when He was called to heal the sore vexed lunatic boy whom His disciples could not cure. "How long," He said, "shall I be with you? How long shall I suffer you?" It was not long. Jerusalem was near, and the end of His sufferings was at hand.

XV

THE PREVISION OF THE CROSS

"He set His face stedfastly to go to Jerusalem."

"The long self-sacrifice of life."
TENNYSON.

CHAPTER XV

THE PREVISION OF THE CROSS

AN attempt has been made to show that our Lord was one manner of man at the outset of His ministry, and another towards its close. According to this theory, His early years were steeped in the sunshine; later on He became a bent and sombre man, the old joy crushed out of His heart by a desire for self-immolation. But to those who accept the gospel histories, nothing can be clearer than that the Cross with its dark shadow lies upon them from the very beginning. The shadow of that Cross is over His cradle, and even in the tranquil years of His childhood and youth it is not absent. An old legend describes Him as working out His own cross in the carpenter's shop at Nazareth. The gospel is like one of those great tragedies where in the earlier scenes a suspicion is infused of the darkness that deepens round the close. The Cross is always present from the very first, although more fully unveiled as time proceeds. The life of Jesus was a perpetual going forth to the Cross.

Else how explain the words which He used at the very beginning of His ministry, to say nothing of the apparent shrinking at Cana? What else can be made of the words, "Destroy this Temple, and in three days I will build it up," and His saying to Nicodemus, "As Moses lifted up the serpent in the wilderness, even so must the Son of man be lifted up"? He said this at the very beginning of His career as Messiah, well knowing, even when things around Him seemed to foretell a different issue, what the end would be.

He tells the happy company that gathered around Matthew's table that a day was coming when a shadow should be thrown over their joy by the taking away of Himself the Bridegroom. And as the close comes nearer, He is still clear and certain in His prediction of the same thing. He knows it as truly in the heyday of His popularity as He knows it when friends forsake Him and enemies are fiercest. He takes His disciples aside and tells them what was to be. He knows not merely the general fact of His death, but its place, its circumstances, and its instruments. He is to die in Jerusalem, for it cannot be that a prophet should perish otherwhere. He is to suffer many things at the hands of the elders and chief priests and scribes. He is to be betrayed to His death by one of His own apostles. He knows the time; not when Jewish hatred seeks to destroy Him, but at the Passover, that He our Passover may die then, and that then He may institute that feast which is to fill up the long space between the old rite and the perfect banquet of His gathered children above. He knows the implement of His death; it is a Cross on which He is to be lifted up.

This prevision taken by itself involves much. To all men, death is near; to some, obviously very near. But yet, when we begin to conjecture whose turn it will be first, what feverish doubt, what baffled conjecture! How different from the unwavering assurance and superhuman quietness of such words as these: "He shall be delivered to the Gentiles, and shall be mocked and spitefully entreated, and spitted on; and they shall scourge Him and put Him to death"! Again, how was it that He in the very start of His ministry, and not without much temporary encouragement, should be so sure of the issue? Had He lived to encounter the chills and reverses of life, and especially such as come to a reformer, we might in some measure have understood it; but the sworn apostle of a new great cause does not begin his work in a spirit like that. In his young hopefulness he says:

> "They are tired of what is old,
>   We will give it voices new;
> For the half hath not been told
>   Of the beautiful and true."

And, generally, it is only after a long and heart-breaking experience that a man makes up his mind that his work is to be a failure, and that his aim is to be defeated; but Jesus Christ knew that from the very first. There is in Him none of that pathetic confidence of a young reformer, on which we look as on the white plumes and unspotted braveries of an army in march for a field of blood. Again, a reformer, when he saw that the end of all his labour was to be death, might accept that death as a necessary incident in his career. He might say, "My life is the price which I have to pay for uttering the truth, and it so much concerns the world that the truth should be uttered that I am willing to pay that price rather than be silent. In order that my work may be done, I am ready to give up my life." Jesus Christ came into the world to bear witness for the truth, but He did not give His life as a price for the witness-bearing of the truth. If He had pleased, He might have borne the most ample testimony to truth, and delivered His message in its full integrity, and yet kept His life. But He gave His life not because the surrender of His life was the penalty of doing His mission, but because it was the great part of His mission,—the great work which He came to accomplish, the centre of His work for the world, and the indispensable condition of attaining the object for which He came.

For Jesus Christ not only foresaw His own death, —He foresaw it as attended with immense moral and spiritual consequences. His visage was to be marred more than any man's, and His form more than the sons of men; every face was to be turned away from His; but all that was to be in order that grief might turn to Him at last, and that He might bear the heavy load of human sorrows and human sins. He saw clearly that this death of His was to be a creative death,—that the Church was to be built upon it, that pardon and cleansing and strength for the world were to come out of it.

This appears in many things—most clearly in His last Supper. "On the night in which He was betrayed,

He took bread; and when He had given thanks, He brake it, and said, Take, eat; this is my body which is broken for you: this do in remembrance of me. After the same manner also He took the cup, when He had supped, saying, This cup is the New Testament in my blood: this do ye, as oft as ye drink it, in remembrance of me." We might speak of the certain and supernatural prevision which this event shows. Human knowledge could not, certainly, declare that His death was at hand, for the Jews had no power to slay Him, and He had done nothing to excite the enmity of the Romans. This is a clear case of supernatural knowledge. But even more remarkable is the power which He attaches to that death in predicting as He does that the bread and wine broken and poured out then would become His body and blood in some sense to future centuries.

> "Both faith and art have given
> To that one hour, a life of endless rest;
> And still whoe'er would taste the food of heaven
> May to that table come a welcome guest."

There was here not only a lucid prevision of the near future, but also a prevision, as wonderful, of the remote future.[1] How did He anticipate that men in after days would show forth His death? His death was a death of shame and violence. After a life spent in teaching and in doing good, would it not have been far more natural that He would wish to sink the fact of His death, patent as the mark of shame, in the memory of His miracles and of His words? And might it not have been anticipated that His disciples

[1] See Hutton's *Essays*, vol. i. p. 131.

would do the same thing? But what are the facts? They actually revive the memory of His humiliation, and make a sacrament of His shame. Century after century His death is associated with His glory, both in the history of the Church and in the experience of Christians. And when He is commended to those who are ignorant of Him, it is by the preaching of His Cross.

I need not stay to point out all that this involves. It involves, for one thing, the truth of the history; for who would ever have begun such an observance save Jesus Himself? The thought would never have commended itself to men. Some thirty years ago an edict against Christianity was issued in China, of which the following is a part:—

"Were their tale fact, it would still be quite inexplicable. Why should the worshippers of Jesus adore the instrument of His punishment, and consider it so to represent Him as not to venture to tread upon it? Would it be common sense, if the father or ancestor of a house had been killed by a shot from a fowling-piece or by a wound from a sword, that his sons or grandsons should adore the fowling-piece or the sword as their father or ancestor?"

This is an instructive proof of how human wisdom looks at the matter. But the foolishness of God is wiser than men, and the weakness of God is stronger than men.

"I am come," said He, "to send fire on earth; and what if it were already kindled?" When the vision of the work which He was to accomplish in the world rose before the Saviour's soul, there came with it also the thought of the baptism which He had to undergo before that work could be done. "I have a baptism to be baptized with, and how am I straitened till it be accomplished!" But He felt that without going through that baptism the work could not be done,— that He had to die before that fire could be kindled which was to warm and purify the world.

2. Along with this prevision of the Cross there was an obvious shrinking from it. This appears, we believe, even at Cana; and in almost every reference to the coming death the same thing is visible. When He sat at the supper table, He could not bear the shadow of Judas lying over the board, and said to him, "That thou doest, do quickly." The words were spoken, no doubt, to get rid of the traitor for the moment, but was there not also the desire to have the slow hours of His agony hastened—to have the time brought near when all should be accomplished?

In another place He says, "How am I straitened till it be accomplished!" as if He were a man held up between two walls, who has no liberty, and who longs to be free. He knows that He cannot be free—that His spirit must be bound and shadowed till that suffering comes, till that restraint is over.

Then, again, we read of Him on His last journey from Jericho to Jerusalem striding up the rocky steeps, with the timid disciples following Him, alarmed at the intense resolve that was marked upon His face. He struggles with and overcomes that reluctance finally at Gethsemane, as we see farther on.

This shrinking also requires explanation, and only

one explanation will meet the facts. Was it the mere shrinking of the physical nature? We shall find it hard to vindicate His manhood if we explain it; but the suggestion may be dismissed without ceremony. No; there is something more. Christ had every reason to wish to be away. We know that He came from the glory which was with the Father, and we know that He was weary of the contradiction of sinners here. "How long time," He said to Philip, "have I been with you?" although it had been but a few months. "The happy hear no clock,"[1] but He, an exile, longed for His home. Why, then, should He shrink from entering it, even though sharp pains had to be passed through before the entrance was accomplished? Why should He not say with His apostle, only with far more clearness, "I am ready to be offered up; the time of my departure is at hand; I have fought a good fight; I have finished the course; I have kept the faith"? Why should He say, instead of that, "My soul is exceeding sorrowful, even unto death"? Because He was bowed down by the burden of the sin of the world.

3. We find that this shrinking is mastered by His fixed and firm resolve. He died of His own free will. Knowing all things that should come upon Him, He nevertheless set His face stedfastly to go to Jerusalem. He not only endured the sufferings that were by the way, but every step was as it were an agony. It was said of Wellington, "The long self-sacrifice of life is o'er"; but this is true strictly of Christ, and of

[1] Schiller.

Christ alone, for His life was a continual going forth to the Cross. If He pleased, He might have escaped it. He did not need to go to Jerusalem; but He went there, and everything that He could do He did to draw attention to Him. He might have averted enmity by silence; but instead of that, He loads His words more and more heavily with denunciation and rebuke. He might have struck His enemies to the ground, or rather kept them on the ground when they fell after coming forward to seize Him. A very slight concession to popular clamour would have saved His life. Nay, even after He had been nailed to the Cross, He might have lived had He pleased. "They bound Him," says Jeremy Taylor, "with cords, but He was bound fast by bonds of His own." He was held by His Father's will, by love of the Father, by love of the world, by ancient prophecies and mysteries of love. Even at the last His death is voluntary; for He cries with a loud voice,—not gasping out words for the strained ear of affection amid the awful silence, —and says, "Father, into thy hands I commend my spirit," and sends away the spirit, death being obedient to Him even when He is obedient to death.

The processes of His mind are strikingly illustrated by John, who describes Greek proselytes coming from a distance asking to see Him. They were strangers to the apostles, and were a testimony of how far and how deep His word had gone. He saw in them the first-fruits of a great harvest, but along with it the augury which it gives of His own death, and comforts Himself by saying, "Except a corn of wheat fall into the ground and die, it abideth alone; but if it die, it bringeth forth much fruit." After He said that, His soul was troubled with the dread of death. But a voice from heaven strengthened Him, and He reasserted the glorious results of His suffering. He was to become the plague of death, and the destruction of the grave, by dying. His death was to be the casting out of the prince of the world, and therefore He set His face stedfastly to go to the Cross.

XVI
JUDAS ISCARIOT

"**Judas Escariot, which also betrayed Him.**"

"Judas, dost thou betray me with a kiss?
Canst thou find hell about my lips, and miss
Of life just at the gates of life and bliss?"
                                    GEORGE HERBERT.

CHAPTER XVI

JUDAS ISCARIOT

THE character of Judas, and our Lord's choice of him as an apostle, form one of the most difficult problems of the gospel history. Without professing to solve it, we shall endeavour to gather the scattered lights, and to learn some of the lessons of this man's life.

He was of Kerioth, the only Judean amongst the apostles, all the rest being Galileans. He might thus look more than they to a temporal kingdom, and the anticipation of a temporal reward would no doubt be a powerful factor in bringing him to the side of Christ. But, besides this, there must have been in him something that was touched by Christ — an emotional element in his nature which the words of Christ reached and moved. Christ would choose those as His apostles who showed outwardly the greatest aptitude in absorbing and teaching the truth of His kingdom, and Judas was in all likelihood previously a disciple of John, and had thus made considerable progress.

This impression is confirmed by the behaviour of the disciples. At first Judas was pleased with Jesus. The early ministry in Galilee, the multitudes, and the miracles, satisfied him. All seemed working towards that end which he most desired; all was harmony and content in the little company, and Judas was made custodian of the small means which all would be expecting soon and greatly to increase. No doubt Judas had this probable increase in view when he sought and accepted the office.

So far all fared well. Judas was never true at heart, but as yet he had not admitted to himself that he was a traitor. All were deceived except Jesus. From the very beginning He knew that Judas had not the root of the matter in him. There was no visible sign of this; and as often an appearance of goodwill is maintained between men who are separated in reality by a sense of moral antagonism, though the rift was there, and daily widening, outsiders supposed them to be good friends.

The first thing that embittered Judas may have been the discourse of Christ on the bread of life, which drove away determined believers, and staggered even the twelve. By this time the process of deterioration had begun, and the door had been widened by inward corruption for the entrance of outward temptation. Judas, being doubtful of a heavenly reward, had begun to steal from the bag; and in the days of Christ's popularity there may have been something to steal. This suspiciousness of Judas, and his consciousness of guilt, must have explained to him the predictions of Christ's death, which the other disciples in their simplicity could not understand. He understood, and hated Christ with an intensified bitterness, because of the downfall of his hopes. This downfall made him desperate. The other disciples had to fight the battle between their old convictions and the new revelation, and the true love in their hearts for Christ enabled them to win the day. Judas, having nothing to resist with, was easily conquered. When the woman, in her lavish kindness, poured the great offering upon Christ, we are told that the disciples said, "To what purpose is this waste?" It was Judas who first made this unworthy and ungenerous speech, and the rest followed him in it, a fact which may be taken as showing both his influence over them, and the imperfection which led them to such a mean and unintelligent appreciation of deeds of love.

Thus far we have seen that he was a thief, and that his hopes were disappointed. Something more follows. Judas was an able man, with a talent for organising, but that talent was not recognised by his being put at the head of the twelve. Peter, James, and John were set above him, and were but ill able to bear this elevation. Peter took the Lord to task because of His announcement that He was to go to Jerusalem and be killed. He evidently thought that Christ was the victim of a morbid hour,—that His spirits had fallen, and that He was forecasting all manner of gloomy things which would never come to pass. James and John tried to entrap their Master into granting unto them whatsoever they should desire, as much as saying, "Promise to give us whatever we ask, then we will tell what it is we are wanting." A number of dissensions on this miserable subject of priority took place amongst the twelve. On the way back from their journey to Cæsarea Philippi, where He seems to have taken them to break to them, aside from all their wonted haunts, the tidings of His death, there was such a dispute. When He got home, He asked them what they had been disputing about. They made no reply. Jesus took a child and set him in the midst of them, and told them that without the spirit of little children they could not enter into the kingdom of heaven. Peter asked how often he should forgive his brother if he sinned against him, and got for his answer, "Seventy times seven." This question would not have been put had it not been that some one had been trying Peter's patience. Who more likely to have done so than Judas? and what more likely to have been the reason than the place which was allotted to Peter amongst the twelve?[1]

There was also a strife at supper amongst the twelve, the occasion probably being that the whole Paschal arrangements were committed to two, and that thus jealousy was roused. Still Judas continued to keep his character, and was sent to preach and heal like the rest. Judas cast out devils, Judas preached the gospel of the kingdom perhaps as eloquently and successfully as any of the band; but whatever were the wonderful works which he wrought, he never truly knew the divine Master.

Jealousy, covetousness, and resentment had been opening the door for the devil. It would not be true to attribute his downfall merely to the love of money. Covetousness is a sin which always brings on others, but here it did not stand alone. His heart was ulcerated by the resentment he felt at Christ—resent-

[1] See a very able paper on Judas by Principal Brown in the *Sunday Magazine*, 1867.

ment that Christ had not fulfilled his hopes, resentment rising from the feeling that Christ knew him thoroughly—the fierce hatred which an impure spirit bears to a pure spirit that knows it. He was also jealous of the rest of the disciples, and lonely in the little band, for nothing isolates a man like a secret sin. These things opened the door of his heart for the entrance of the Wicked One. Satan entered first by inspiring a thought, then by turning that thought into a settled purpose, and last by giving an occasion for the fulfilment of that dark resolve. The rebuke administered to him by Christ in connection with Mary no doubt crystallised his evil purpose; and just at that moment, when the chief priests were discussing how Jesus could be taken in the crowded city without rousing the ire of the people, with whom He was popular, Judas presented himself, and offered to do the deed for thirty pieces of silver.

He had two days to reconsider it, and we find that Jesus, who till now had encompassed him with His serene though grave regard, began specially to deal with his conscience. Still he did not quail. He sat down at the supper table, and allowed Jesus to wash his feet. The Saviour could scarcely endure such hardened hypocrisy, and said, "Ye are not all clean." He was troubled by the presence of Judas, wanted him away, and said, "One of you shall betray me." He gave him a sop, which the others interpreted as a mark of affection. Judas was not even yet ripe, so Satan entered into him. Jesus could bear it no longer, and said, "That thou doest, do quickly." The disciples did not understand; Judas understood, and went out, and it was night—night overhead, and a deeper night in his guilty soul.

Jesus was now alone with His disciples, and never did He speak greater and sweeter words than those which He uttered in that night of sorrow and weakness and love. The many mansions of His Father's house rose for them in their unfading serenity. He told them of His own abiding presence, and of the gift of His Spirit, and spoke words that are almost the dearest of all to the Christian heart. He then went out, fought the battle of Gethsemane, and won the victory in His soul. It is Judas' time now: "Whomsoever I shall kiss, the same is He; hold Him fast." Casting the last particle of restraint away, he kisses Him. Even then Jesus does not quite abandon him. "Comrade, wherefore art thou come? Comrade,"—striking on the chord of old companionship, "by all the memory of our time together, by all the memory of my deeds and words, and your professions, I ask you, are you to persevere in this?" Then, "Wherefore art thou come?"—striking the conscience, asking Judas even yet to give his deed a name, in the hope that when he had named it, he would shrink from a crime so foul. In vain; Jesus is betrayed; Judas receives the bribe. The bribe, instead of comforting, torments him. There are quaint mediæval stories written with a recollection of this,—one of a sorcerer who gave bags of gold to his tools, and when they went next day to spend their gold, they found the bags full of leaves; another of a magician who used to receive men and horses in his castle, and entertain them sumptuously, but after their meal they were immediately torn with the pangs of hunger. Judas' bribe ate his flesh like fire. He came with it to the chief priests, and received the answer, "What is that to us?" If he had but gone with his sin to Christ, who never said to anyone who came with his sin and burden, "What is that to me?" how different might the result have been! But his betrayers had no word of comfort for him, so he flung the silver pieces on the floor of the Temple, and departed, and went and hanged himself.

The character of Judas is no doubt a difficult problem, but there are materials that help us to a comprehension of it. He was, to begin with, a man of emotion. How precarious that is let his history tell. He had been touched by the words of Christ, and his faculty of impressibility gave him a certain aptness both to receive and to teach. But his fate shows how little emotion is when not issuing from principle. He was an able man, for he to some extent controlled the rest of the disciples, and—a more difficult task—largely controlled himself. What immense self-possession and determination is shown in the record of his life! But he was covetous, and that sin eats away and destroys all nobleness. There must have been something singularly loathsome in the man who could betray his Master for a bribe and with a kiss. Again, he was an apostate, and there is not bitterness like the bitterness of a traitor. And we touch an element which we cannot explain, when we say that in this way the doors were thrown open, for the devil came in, and the unhappy man was led captive by Satan at his will.

An attempt has been made to show that the character of Judas was much higher than has been commonly believed—that he was the victim of a misconception, and that he hoped to do Christ good by betraying Him. Against this is the irresistible evidence of Christ's own description. He says that Judas is a devil, and that it had been better for him that he had never been born. Words of "immeasurable ruin, of immeasurable woe!" The only colourable pretext for the theory is that Judas committed suicide; and it is said that this shows him to be a nobler man than if he had remained an honoured leader amongst the Pharisees, dying in the odour of sanctity. But this rests on an assumption. It may be admitted that the lowest type of criminal is the callous wretch who commits crimes and justifies them, or feels that they need no justification. Such a one, however, is of a lower type originally than Judas, who, as we have admitted, must have had originally an element of nobleness and generosity in his character. This original endowment does not make Judas' crime less but more, because, if it is granted, Judas fell from a greater eminence. Further, this theory assumes that it is by inward workings of conscience that a man perceives sin; but are there not some sins so gigantic as to force themselves upon conscience once they take shape? and was not this one of them? There are sins which, once committed, stand out in glaring and appalling clearness to the dullest eyes. *When he saw—* when the sin stared him in the face, it was so terrible that Judas could not endure the sight, and he plunged into the thick darkness of eternity.

The character of Judas throws a vivid light on the life of Christ. What must it have been for Him constantly to endure the presence of such a one? Many a reformer, whose name outside has been a lightning-rod for storms to strike on, has been upheld by this, that he had a refuge at home, where all things were looked on in the soft light of love. It was part of Christ's suffering that He had no such place, that He constantly had to endure the presence of a traitor, that in His most intimate and confidential moments this presence was there to mar the happiness. What patience is manifest in His treatment of Judas! Though He knew who should betray Him, He teaches him, pleads with him, seems even to have hope for him to the very last. Not till the very last does He let him go. When His agonies are thick upon Him, and His foes are near, He makes one last attempt to win Judas' hard heart, "Comrade, wherefore art thou come?"

Then, what inexpressible force there is in the testimony of Judas to Christ! He had watched Him with fierce, prejudiced, suspicious eyes. It might have saved his life if he could have brought to mind one word, one deed of Christ's, to give the least excuse for his crime; but he could find none. He thought over all in vain; and so he confesses, "I have betrayed innocent blood." The confession is extorted even from his lips, and if from his lips, sooner or later it must be from all lips: "I find no fault in Him."

XVII
GETHSEMANE

"*Who in the days of His flesh, when He had offered up prayers and supplications, with strong crying and tears, unto Him that was able to save Him from death, and was heard in that He feared.*"

"Strange was His birth—His death and rising such
As to bear out that strangeness—and as much
May well be said of dark Gethsemane,
That sternest link in the great unity."
CHARLES TURNER.

CHAPTER XVII

GETHSEMANE

THE agony of Gethsemane is one of the most prominent, and at the same time one of the most mysterious, passages in our Lord's life. We find it recorded in more or less detail in no fewer than three of the evangelists. Besides, in the Epistle to the Hebrews the narrative is commented upon, and one vivid and impressive detail is added. We are told that Jesus in the days of His flesh offered prayers and supplications, with strong crying and tears, unto Him that was able to save from death, and was heard in that He feared. That strong crying and tears were the accompaniments of His prayers, we know only from the Epistle, and the detail is used to show the reality of the Lord's priesthood, and its help for us in our struggles and sorrows. The explanation of the scene, however, takes us much further, although this element must not be omitted. Gethsemane was a place near Jerusalem, where the Saviour often resorted to pray with His disciples. His oratory was to be the scene of His sharpest conflict and suffering. There still stand olive trees which may have succeeded those that saw the supreme agony of Christ.

The suffering at Gethsemane was evidently of peculiar intensity. Jesus was familiar with the varied forms of suffering, and His biographers with their recital. Many and keen were the pangs of the chastisement of our peace that had gone before, but apparently they were far transcended here. Very unusual words are employed to describe this centre and heart of His suffering, as if language were taxed to convey an adequate expression. He was sore amazed. He was very heavy. His soul was exceeding sorrowful, even to the point of death, as if any addition to the burden would have been enough to snap the breaking thread of life. He prayed with strong crying and tears to Him who was able to save Him from death, and was heard in that He feared. This was no torture of the body, no physical agony, but the far keener pains of the spirit. The fastidious reticence of modern times must not prevent us looking at the stern and naked reality which is with a very gracious intent disclosed to us. The suffering was so sacred, that, though He was glad to feel His disciples near, He could not bear them so near that they should see it, and said, "Sit ye here, while I go and pray yonder." But we are taken into the most sacred ground. It was needful that we should see the agony of His spirit. Had we not witnessed this great and solitary expression of pain, we would have been in danger of supposing that His divinity made the fact of His suffering less precious and less helpful to us. We might have said, "God cannot suffer as I suffer. His pains are not to Him what mine are to me." And it is that this doubt should be for ever silenced that the veil is lifted, and our eyes behold His awful agony, His bloody sweat, His great heaviness, His sore amazement, His strong crying and tears. His suffering, though in one sense quite unique, is, we are warranted in believing, a guide and a solace for us when a sorrow comes which makes us solitary, and renders unavailing the sympathy that helps us in our common woes. As there come times sooner or later when no human sympathy is enough,—bereavements which no human love can supply, wounds which the closest affection cannot stanch,—when nothing really helps but the sympathy of Christ, —this assures us that He can sympathise even as He suffered, that He can go with us down the loneliest road of sorrow and of loss, because His feet have gone even farther, and His footprints are seen stretching away to the darkness beyond it. There is a Roman story of a husband and wife, who, weary of this tyrant-ridden world, resolved to commit suicide. The wife took the blade and plunged it into her breast, and then drew it out, saying with her dying breath, "Take it; it is not painful." So, when the dagger of sorrow is plunged into our hearts, it is tinctured with the blood of Christ. It has gone into Christ's heart before it was plunged into ours, and this has robbed it of its keenest agony. So, when we have no other companion, we are able to flee to Him and to say, "He learned obedience by the things which He suffered, and, being made perfect, He became the author of eternal salvation to all them that obey Him." As the intensity of the agony grew greater, and He felt Himself dying, He asked whether the cup might not be foregone.

He made His last appeal to the Fatherly love and omnipotence of God: "Abba, Father, all things are possible unto thee." He did not abandon the salvation of the world, but He asked whether this cup, so bitter and terrible, must be drunk in order to accomplish it. Three times He prayed, and as He prays He grows more resigned. "He was heard," says the inspired writer, "in that He feared"; in other words, He was heard for His piety—His submissive reverence. His submissive reverence appeared in that He said, "Father, if it be possible"; and again in that He said, "Not my will, but thine be done. If it be possible, in thine unlimited power, canst thou not find another way? Nevertheless, not my will, but thine be done." There is no revolt; He is ready to accept the answer, whatever it may be. There is the reluctance of the flesh, — the drawing back of humanity — the resistance of natural instinct, — but that is all. In all His purpose He never faltered, never ceased to be the Son. The will of nature did not for a moment escape from the law of the Spirit, and after a struggle it was entirely absorbed in it. There was the conflict between resignation and emotion. Resignation does not mean the suppression of human and natural feeling. There may be true reverence, and humble submission, and a faithful acceptance of all the sorrow and defeat that life brings, and that God sends, and yet at the same time there may be sorrow, and the distinct expression of sorrow, without sin. There is no sin in the strong crying; no irreligion in the tears. It was right that He should suffer; it was right to express the suffering, so that He was able to say in the end, "Not my will, but thine be done." "I was dumb; I opened not my mouth, because thou didst it, till the light came at last, and I was able to say, 'The Lord gave, and the Lord hath taken away; blessed be the name of the Lord.'" When we lose our friends, even though we know that they have cast off for ever the burden of humanity, and have entered into the peace of God, we yet may rightly go to the grave in mourning and weep there. Strong crying and tears are part of our agony, and it is not God's mind that we should affect a composure that we do not feel. He has patience with our tears, so long as they mean no wandering of the heart and will—so long as the sorrow is bounded by submission, and does not become bitter and rebellious.

Again, as there was a conflict between submission and sorrow, there was a conflict between inclination and duty. They ran counter, as they must often, and there was no sin in the conflict. His nature rose up within Him against the punishment. The body and soul protested against the thought of suffering thus. The fact of this natural shrinking is what makes it possible for nature to become the real victim—an offering in earnest. So long as the voice of nature is at one with that of God, it may be asked, "Where is the victim for the burnt-offering?" Sacrifice begins where conflict begins. But the conflict must not be maintained until it turns away the will; and it was not maintained in this case. Duty mastered inclination, submission sorrow—or sorrow was bounded by submission; and thus it was that the answer came, "He was heard because of His piety."

The cup did not pass from Him; it had to be drunk. Not even a drop could be spared. Yet He was heard. The angel appeared from heaven strengthening Him. There would have been not only spiritual consolation, but physical help. The cup was not made sweeter, but His lips were made brave to drink it. The nature of the punishment was not changed, but the thought of it was no longer the same. He accepted the work, and was enabled to walk with a firm step to meet the agony at which He had staggered. Besides, not His will but God's will was done, and that was what He prayed for. By prayer and supplication He had made His request known to God, and the peace that passeth understanding came to Him.

While the incident thus illustrates the reality of His priesthood, and shows with how firm a step He could tread on the narrow and difficult ways that part right from wrong, there needs something more to be said in explanation of all this suffering. He did not endure it merely that He might be able to sympathise with us. How is it to be explained when we look at Him there, shrinking, shuddering, with great drops of sweat mingling with the hot tears that fell on the ground? Is there the demeanour we should expect from the bravest of the brave—from the leader of heroes and martyrs? Is He shrinking under the mere anticipation of physical suffering? If it be so, the servant is above his

Master; for many a poor martyr has gone to his death as to a bed long desired, and many a delicate woman has endured as much bodily suffering without almost a tear or sob. Is He then agitated with all this terror by the impending suffering which others have borne bravely and calmly? If so, how was it that He was able to carry Himself as He afterwards did? How was He able to bear silently the insults and the tortures of His enemies—to master, with the calm ascendancy of His bearing, His hardened judges? He prayed, when the nails were driven through His hands, "Father, forgive them, for they know not what they do." Why did He so shrink from death, which meant to Him deliverance from the load of humanity, and a resuming of the glory which He had with the Father before the sinful world was? We should have imagined that the agony, great as it was, would have been forgotten and overlooked in the thought of the great bliss that was to follow it. If so, how was it that He did not take a way of escape? A word might have saved Him. Pilate would have been glad of an excuse to set Him free. Without violating truth, He might, one would imagine, have escaped all that which He seemed to fear so much. No, the explanation is utterly inadequate. No mere dread of pain could thus agitate a soul like His. "There is no passion in the mind of man so weak but that it meets and masters the fear of death. A man would die if he were neither valiant nor miserable, only upon the weariness to do the same thing so oft over and over. It is no less worthy to observe how little alteration in good spirits the approaches of death make, for they appear to be the same men till the last instant." It cannot be explained, as some have attempted, by the thought of the desertion of His disciples. To state such an explanation is to refute it. There is only one explanation that will cover the facts: "The Lord laid upon Him the iniquity of us all." He was forsaken by God, He was enduring the punishment of our sins, He was drinking the cup we should have drained, and because our punishment was upon His sinless soul, the waters of His baptism were so deep and chill and black that He feared, and wept, and shuddered before He entered them. Nothing will explain the suffering of Gethsemane except the fact that He died to bear the great burden of sin—our representative, the just for the unjust, that He might bring us to God.

There was something more than anticipation. He freely accepted death as the punishment of sin; and in order to distinguish Him from typical victims, there was needed such an acceptance in the fulness of His consciousness and liberty. But is it true to say, that at Gethsemane Jesus did not drink the cup, but merely consented to drink it? Rather would we say that Gethsemane is the soul of His suffering. He laid down His life in the garden. No man took it from Him; He laid it down of Himself. There was the inner suffering before the outward suffering came. There had to be the outward suffering, for the world could not understand Gethsemane. It must have a historical fact capable of being tested by many witnesses. There must be something literal and clear. So the Cross is lifted up on Calvary, and men see Him nailed there, and His blood is poured out. It is in this way that we are at first led to understand His suffering. We begin with the story of the Cross, and the nails, and the lifting up of the victim, and the nerves quivering, and the life as one pang. But we are led by and by into the inner sanctuary—into the suffering of His soul. The soul of His suffering was the bearing of our sins. And He bore our sins in Gethsemane and on Calvary, and we put the two together to understand His work for us. He rose from Gethsemane when the bitterness of death passed. Resistance is over; He gives Himself up to the ruffian band. Men cross-question Him, buffet Him, drag Him about, but He will never speak a word more. He is led as a lamb to the slaughter, and as a sheep before her shearers is dumb, so He opens not His mouth. He goes on without flinching to bear the full weight of His cross.

XVIII
THE TRIAL OF CHRIST

"As a sheep before her shearers is dumb, so He opened not His mouth."

"My silence rather doth augment their cry,
My dove doth back into my bosom fly,
Because the raging waters still are high."

GEORGE HERBERT.

CHAPTER XVIII

THE TRIAL OF CHRIST

THE death of Christ was the execution of a capital sentence proceeding upon a sixfold trial — three trials at the hands of the Jews, and three at the hands of the Romans. Out of the manifold details given by the evangelists, it is somewhat difficult to reach perfect certainty as to the precise order of events, although the general truthfulness of the narrative is apparent. We attempt to relate the incidents of the successive trials, but every detail cannot be certainly laid down.[1]

He was tried first of all at the hands of the Jews. The Hebrew commonwealth and institutions were pervaded by a deep sentiment of justice. In the traditions of the fathers we read, that when a judge decides not according to truth, he makes the majesty of God depart from Israel. But if he judges according to truth, were it only for one hour, it is as if he established the whole world, for it is in judgment that the divine presence in Israel has its habitation.

[1] See two articles by A. Taylor-Innes in the *Contemporary Review*, vol. xxx., and the brilliant narrative in Farrar's *Life of Christ*.

When Jesus was bound, He was led through the sleeping city to the palace of the High Priest. On the Thursday night He had been arrested, because resistance was looked for, and He was first brought before Annas, who seems to have occupied the High Priest's palace jointly with his son-in-law Caiaphas. Annas was by far the most influential man in the Sanhedrim. He had been for several years High Priest, but had been removed from that office twenty years before, probably for stretching his powers to the extent of executing capital punishment. But he had been succeeded by his own relatives. Five of his sons were members of the Sanhedrim, and either had held, or were to hold, the office of High Priest, while the acting High Priest Caiaphas was his son-in-law. He was regarded by the Jews as High Priest *de jure*, although not High Priest *de facto*. He viewed Jesus with feelings of bitter contempt and hatred, and endeavoured at the very outset to extort from Him admissions which would involve His death. According to the Jewish law, this examination was wholly illegal. The accused was free from all personal investigation until brought to trial before the assembly of his brethren. By the Hebrew law there was no sole judge, and no sole witness. Jesus therefore refused to answer him. "I have in secret said nothing: why askest thou me? ask them which heard me," thus taking His stand on pure Hebrew justice. The minions of Annas felt the force of the reply, and one of them struck Jesus on the face, saying, "Answerest thou the High Priest so?" The contrast between Paul's sudden anger when similarly insulted, and the supernatural calmness of Christ, has been often marked. He again took His stand on His legal rights, and said, "If I have spoken evil, bear witness to the evil; but if not, why smitest thou me?" Annas was baffled, and sent Him on to Caiaphas. Caiaphas, although of the same mind as the father-in-law, was a man of less force of will. He saw that there was no way of getting Jesus condemned without seeking false witness. This was utterly illegal. Hebrew judges were eminently counsel for the accused. To seek out witnesses was a scandalous violation of law. The law was thoroughly violated already by the trial taking place at night. Even an ordinary civil suit should have been confined to the day, and a grave criminal trial could be begun, continued, and finished only in the light. The witnesses were not able to agree. One reported that Jesus had said, "I can destroy the Temple"; another, "I will destroy the Temple." What He actually said was, If the Temple be destroyed, He would build it up. The charge which they were aiming to establish was eminently one of conspiracy against the national institutions, which with them was blasphemy,—a crime coming under the same category as the claim to be the Messiah, or the Son of God. Jesus allowed the false witnesses to confound one another. Their crime was all the greater because of the solemn adjuration the High Priest had to pronounce to them: "In this trial for life, if thou sinnest, the blood of the accused, and the blood of his sin to the end of time, shall be imputed unto thee." He held His peace, and His silence maddened His accusers. He was perfectly self-possessed, for all this had been foreknown to Him, and He had come to Jerusalem, not to perish by mistake, but to die as a Priest. His enemies seemed likely to be baffled, when Caiaphas, overcome with anger and terror, strode into the midst of the hall, and said, "Answerest thou nothing? What is it that these witness against thee?" The silence was unbroken, and then the High Priest exclaimed, "I adjure thee by the living God, that thou tell us whether thou be the Christ, the Son of the Blessed." This was the question for which all had been waiting, and the answer came. Looking at the man who had lifted himself out of the crowd of aged and evil faces, Jesus replied, "I am; and ye shall see the Son of man sitting at the right hand of power, and coming with the clouds of heaven." They tore their clothes, the ordinance in Israel being that every man who heard blasphemy should rend his garments into two parts, never again to be united; and the High Priest exclaimed, "Blasphemy! What further need have we of witnesses? What think ye? He is a man of death."

He had to be kept till break of day, because only by daylight and by a full session of the Sanhedrim could He be legally condemned. It was far past midnight, and the spring air was chill as they led Him, with blows and curses, to the guard-room. As He was led past, He heard Peter denying Him with oaths and curses. This was at the very beginning of the terrible derision, which we cannot bear to describe in detail. Suffice it to say that the worst passions of men were wreaked upon Him. When dawn came, probably about six o'clock in the morning, a full session of the Sanhedrim, almost all against Him, met. He was silent for a time, but again declared Himself at last to be the Son of God. The third condemnation followed, and a second derision resembling the first.

He suffered under Pontius Pilate. The man thus condemned to eternal infamy was at that time the governor of Judea. He had made himself obnoxious to the Jews by a mixture of tyranny and weakness. At the very beginning of his career as procurator, he allowed his soldiers to bring with them the silver eagles, and other insignia of the legions, from Cesarea to the Holy City. This excited a tumult of rebellion, to which he had to give way. Other foolish or malicious deeds had made him very unpopular with the people. He lived during his brief residence at Jerusalem in the gorgeous palace of Herod, one of those luxurious abodes on which skill and wealth had been lavished. That morning he was sitting in his prætorium to do business as usual. He was sitting in his judgment hall, with the altars of the Roman gods in the heathen chamber. The Jews, during the Holy Week, would not enter the place, and he goes out to them in the early sunlight, probably in no good humour. "What accusation bring ye against this Man?"—the voice of Roman justice; for the Romans were distinguished for their instinctive righteousness, their passion for justice. The insolent answer was, "If He were not a malefactor, we would not have delivered Him up to thee." Pilate, refusing to act as executioner where he had not been the judge, contemptuously replies, "Take ye Him and judge Him according to your law." He thus forces them into the sullen confession that they could not put Jesus to death. He was not to die by a Jewish punishment, but by the awful Roman death of the cross. There does not seem to have been any concordat as to the power of death between the Jews and the Romans. They dropped the charge of blasphemy, which would have availed them nothing before Pilate, and urged that Jesus had perverted the nation, forbidding to give tribute to Cæsar, and saying that He Himself was the Christ the King. Pilate took Jesus into his hall, and asked Him, "Art thou the King of the Jews?" There might have been a pitying wonder, and yet at the same time an instinctive reverence for the nobleness of the prisoner in the question, "Art thou, pale, spent, weary man, art thou the King of the Jews?" Jesus replies, "Sayest thou this of thyself, or did others tell it thee of me?" evidently meaning, In what sense is the expression used? "If thou sayest of thyself as a Roman would use the expression, I am not; but if thou art using the words of Hebrew prophecy, I have something further to explain." Pilate replies, "I am not a judge. Thine own nation and the chief priests have delivered thee to me; what hast thou done?" Christ, in reply, explained that He was a King, but that His kingdom was not of this world. He acknowledged that a kingdom of this world might be legitimately attacked by the deputy of Cæsar, but such a kingship He did not claim. "Art thou a King, then?" said the Roman; and the answer was, "I am a King, and I was born to bear witness to the truth." "Truth," replied Pilate, "what is truth?"—strange mixture of impatience, sarcasm, and despair. The prisoner before him, he thought, was not one likely to interfere with any existing royalty. He was an innocent and high-souled dreamer—nothing more. So Pilate went out to the Jews, and emphatically acquitted Him: "I find in Him no fault at all."

If he had but kept to this verdict; but the fury of the people burst out. Was the judgment of the High Priest to be frustrated by this heathen? Jesus had troubled the people through the whole land, beginning from Galilee; and Pilate, eager to catch at every pretext, sends Jesus to Herod Antipas, the tetrarch of Galilee, who was then in Jerusalem. Jesus was dragged through the streets before the bar of this wretched debauchee, who had murdered John the Baptist. Of Herod Jesus had used the only contemptuous expression He ever employed. Now He looked at him for the first time face to face. Herod put many questions. He had no remorse for what had been. He hoped that Jesus would amuse him by some miracle. When Jesus confronted him with silence, the savagery of the man broke through his voluble good-nature, and he and his minions treated Jesus with contempt and insult, and sent Him back again to Pilate. It was right that a man accused of treason should be judged at Cæsar's judgment-seat. In the meantime Pilate had received a message from his wife. She had been visited in her dream by the thought that the blood of that just person would be required of her husband,

and in her restless anxiety she sent to let him know. With the superstition that often goes along with scepticism, Pilate was troubled, and sought again to save himself from the guilt of condemning Jesus. He summoned the priests and people before him, told them that their charges had absolutely broken down, but, willing to go half way with them, ordered Jesus to be scourged publicly, and further proposed to set free at the paschal feast, when a condemned prisoner was always liberated, Jesus Christ. The people would not accept the compromise. They clamoured for the liberation of Barabbas, a murderer and a thief, whose sedition had made him popular amongst them. Jesus was rejected of men. "What then," said Pilate, "shall I do with Him?" The mad cry came, "Crucify Him, crucify Him!" Before that crucifixion the awful agony of scourging had to come, according to the cruel customs of the Romans, almost alone among civilised nations in this. They put a crown of thorns round Him, and arrayed Him in a purple robe, putting a reed sceptre in His hands, and crying derisively, "Hail, King of the Jews." Pilate even yet hoped to save Him. He led Jesus—in the sad finery with which they had tricked Him out, with the marks of indignity upon Him—and showed Him to the people, saying, "Behold the Man!" Still they insisted, "We have a law, and by our law He ought to die, because He made Himself the Son of God." That word "Son of God" startled Pilate. He took Him into the hall again, and asked Him, "Whence art thou?" Jesus was silent, and Pilate flashed out insolently with the question, "Speakest thou not unto me? Knowest thou not that I have power to crucify thee, and power to release thee?" Jesus replies gently, "Thou couldest have no power at all over me, unless it were given thee from above; therefore he that delivered me unto thee hath the greater sin." Jesus judges His judge tenderly yet truly: "Thy crime is great, but the crime of Annas, Caiaphas, Judas, the priests, and Jews, is greater still." Pilate would make one more effort. He brings Him out again, and cries, "Behold your King!" By this time the conflict had lasted some hours, and the people were passionate and weary. "Shall I crucify your King?" said he. "We have no king," the reply was, "but Cæsar; and if thou let this man go, thou art not Cæsar's friend." Pilate was paralysed with terror at the awful name of Tiberius. Was he to be accused before that man, with whom the accusation of treason was almost certain death—who at that time, full of ulcers and fevers and leprosy, maddened by the treason of his only friend, was waiting for opportunities for new infamies? He yielded; but his conscience was reproaching him, and, in the vain attempt to appease it, he went through the farce of washing his hands: "I am innocent of the blood of this just person; see you to it." They accepted the burden of the awful guilt, and answered him back with a yell, "His blood be upon us and our children!" Pilate delivered Him unto them that He might be crucified.

1. The great importance of the trial for our purpose lies in the fact that the issue raised was Christ's claim to be the Son of God, the Messiah of Israel, and a

King. He was tried unfairly and judged unjustly, but the true issue was raised. He died, then, because before the Jews He claimed to be the Son of God and the Messiah, and before Pilate to be Christ and King.

2. All generations since have felt that the judged was the judge. The men were really standing before the bar of Christ, and all appear in terrible distinctness, revealed by the Light of the world. Pilate, with his proud indifference to the superstitions of the Jews, his contempt for the High Priests, his scorn for the mob, his supercilious wonder at Christ's mysticism and impracticability, his clear recognition of the nobleness behind these, his uneasy attempts to get quit of responsibility and pacify the conscience, which troubled while it did not rule him, by catching at spray after spray, and finally his yielding—overborne though unconvinced—of Jesus to be crucified; firm only in refusing to blot out the title written in scorn, and yet with unconscious truth, over His head; all these are unmistakable. Caiaphas, seeing his occasion in the terror of the nation that the Romans might efface them, and urging that this victim would appease the suspicion of their conquerors, and preserve the nation,—a consideration so important as to make it of no consequence whether He was innocent or not,—is a type of one who misinterprets the divine covenant which he represented. Herod, with selfish and sensual goodnature, thinly veiling ferocity and heartlessness, seeking to have miracles performed to gratify his appetite for physical marvel, and treating Christ's silence as a proof of His imposture, shows the end of a man in whom

conscience is dead. John the Baptist, if he thought of him at all, would seem much superior to this dumb coward, who could not make a king tremble.

And Jesus, what shall we say of Him? The great characteristic of the history is missed in reading it, for the events pass quickly in the terse narrative. It is the almost utter silence before all the judges, and the complete passiveness in the hands of those who insulted— all this, accompanied, as has been truly imagined, by a look not of fortitude and tension, but rather of recollection, as if there was nothing in all these insults and questions to which any answer or expostulation was appropriate, but rather a current of inevitable passions which must be, but the moving spring of which is beyond the reach of words. No morbid dejection, no personal resentment, but a complete detachment from all earthly passion, and at the same time a conscious drawing out of deep springs of strength and consolation, which no human malice could reach to choke— infinitely above them all, their Judge while they judged Him.

XIX
THE SEVEN WORDS ON THE CROSS

"**Truly this was the Son of God.**"

——— - —

"In the wild heart of that eclipse
These words came from his wasted lips."

ALEXANDER SMITH.

CHAPTER XIX

THE CROSS AND THE SEVEN WORDS

WE do not attempt to describe the physical sufferings of Christ upon the Cross. Yet to describe, and in certain cases even to dwell upon these, is not only warrantable but dutiful. While it would be utterly wrong and needless to add any touch or colour of horror, yet it is not without reason that the Gospels, which hurry over our Lord's life so rapidly, here take the minuteness of diaries, describing every incident and noting every word. The insulting voices, the racked frame, the fiery thirst, the last atrocity of crucifixion—these, and much else, are not described without reason. They were foretold in prophecy. And though it might seem as if human passion had been let loose to have its will with Him, yet even in its madness it was controlled by a divine hand, and could go thus far and no farther. But we propose to omit these things, needful though it be to make much of them at times to "scarify callosities," and to teach sentimentalists, who see or wear the Cross glittering in jewels, how terrible was the reality, and how deep and awful is the meaning of the commandment which bids us take up our cross. No reaction from the sensational preaching once, at least, prevalent in the Church of Rome, should prevent this.

But we pass it by to dwell upon the seven words uttered on the Cross, which are as seven windows through which we may gaze at the soul of Christ.

Last words are always earnestly heeded—

> "The tongues of dying men
> Enforce attention like deep harmony;
> When words are scarce they're seldom spent in vain,
> For they breathe truth that breathe their words in pain."

Especially memorable and solemn are the last words of Christ—the few utterances amidst the long silence of that half day He hung upon the Cross. The absorbing and confounding agonies of crucifixion do not disturb the order and the calm which marked all His life. As He had done all things fitly in the calmer spaces of His life, and in the three years of conflict, so now He does all things well in the midst of this awful battle on the Cross. Seven times His lips are opened. Not surely without a reason is the number chosen. There is sevenfold completeness in His utterances. We trace an order and progress in these seven utterances. All His life through He had thought first of His enemies and last of Himself. He came to call sinners to repentance. When the pains of death got hold on Him in the midst of His grief and trouble, He remained the same. His first thought was for His enemies, His last for Himself. We find Him thinking first of His enemies, next of an enemy who had become a friend, next of a friend, and so narrowing the circle, He comes to Himself last of all.

1. "Father, forgive them, for they know not what

they do." He said it after a night of mortal agony, after six successive trials, after Roman scourging and mocking, while the rough nails were being driven through His hands. The horror of it all overwhelms Him. He has no thought of His own agony, but much of His murderers' guilt; and therefore are His lips opened in prayer.

It is much to be able to pray in great agony of body; it is more to feel the Fatherhood of God as He felt it. He had said "Father" in the morning of His life, through it all, and now in the black midnight it is "Father" once again. His faith does not fail, will not fail for all the powers of darkness, howsoever they enshroud Him. But most wonderful of all is it that He prayed not for Himself, not for the mitigation of His suffering, nor for any beloved friend, but for His enemies, in the height of their crime. "Father," He says, "forgive them," by that blood which is already flowing through their cruelty, "for they know not what they do." The awfully suggestive reason tells us that we never see sin as He saw it from the tree of the Cross. If they had known it, as Paul says in an awestruck undertone, they would not have crucified the Lord of glory. When we sin, we never know what we do. We throw at a mark, and know not that the missiles pass beyond our reach; they go higher than we meant—they strike God, and He from His Cross saw them reach that goal.

"They know not what they do." He knew, and He could pray for forgiveness. They were not guiltless. Ignorance is not innocence, else they had not needed pardon. They knew cruelty and torture to be wicked, and they might have known more of Him whom they were crucifying. Still, in the divine view, their ignorance was some palliation. Indeed, it is not too much to say that our ignorance is our hope. If we had sinned like the rebel angels, in the full light of heaven, our case would have been different. But because we have not, we dare to hope that He says for us, "Father, forgive them, for they know not what they do."

2. Having prayed for His enemies who were persecuting Him and crucifying Him, He speaks to one who had been a great enemy, but who was now a friend: "To-day shalt thou be with me in Paradise." Two thieves were crucified with Him; one on His right hand, and the other on His left. One reviled Him, but the other rebuked his companion, and bore witness to the innocent Lord by saying, "We are paying for our sins, but this man hath done nothing amiss." Then he prayed, "Lord, remember me when thou comest unto thy kingdom."

This story must be true, for it never could have been imagined. These words so stand out as to be their own best testimony. Who could have invented such a prayer? "Lord," he said, seeing the Lord in the victim. When all were mocking and deriding the Saviour, and when the other thief was calling upon Him to take Himself and them from the Cross, this robber saw a greater nobility in His continuing to hang there, read aright the words written over His head, and trusted Him through all the scorn as "Lord." At the very depth of His suffering this malefactor saw

Christ to be a King. He saw the crown through the Cross, and declared, "He hath done nothing amiss." When no mouth was opened to testify for Christ, His defence was spoken by this strange tongue. Those held their peace, and this stone immediately cried out. But more : he knew the Lord not only as King, but as Redeemer. "Remember me," he said. What a perfectly brave word of love ! Throwing his heart at the feet of the omniscient Lord, he said, "Remember all my spent, bad past : how I began to sin, how I went on from one wickedness to another till I came where I am; do not forget anything, but remember with it all that I trusted thee." He was not afraid that the Lord should know all things when He knew that He loved him; he had no doubt of the length, and breadth, and depth, and height of the infinite love which went beyond the robber's life. "I have no fear to tell you what I was, being what I am," says an English poet; so the penitent thief says, "I have no fear of all my past, being what I am, a penitent believer." Besides, he saw the kingdom beyond the Cross. He did not ask to be taken down from the Cross, but, "When this darkness is over, and we emerge into the light, Lord, remember me."

How grateful must this testimony and this prayer have been to Christ ! The story is like a flower of beauty amongst those dreary crags of agony. This was the last tongue that had a word to say for Him. On the Cross He saw somewhat of the travail of His soul, and His dying eyes were satisfied ere they closed. How quick was the answer, "To-day shalt thou be with me in Paradise"! "To-day!"—that very word was a gospel. He was not to hang for long hours in agony, as many did; but "To-day"—he was to escape—"shalt thou be with me in Paradise"; Lord and thief together. We may suppose that he did not understand much of the word "in Paradise," any more than we do; but he understood the word "with me," and it was enough. Jesus said it from His Cross: "But thus saith He that is holy, He that is true, He that hath the key of David, He that openeth and no man shutteth, and shutteth and no man openeth." The prayer was great, but the answer was greater still. If the prayer was like a river, the answer was as a great sea.

3. Next He speaks to a friend: "Woman, behold thy son; son, behold thy mother!" He looked from the Cross, and coming from the outer circle, nearer to His heart, He saw His mother and the beloved disciple standing by, and He commended them to one another.

Every commentator has rightly pointed out the tenderness of those words. But, as has been noted before, there is something in the relation between Christ and His mother which is not to be explained on the supposition that He was merely her human son. The mere affection shown her does not surprise us: rather do we wonder at the reticence of His words. She stood there, with the sword of prophecy piercing her heart, in unutterable woe, and He says no more than, "Woman, behold thy son." The hour of death has been called—

> "That dark hour when bands remove,
> And none are named but names of love."

And we have all known how even the most stern, unbending, and rugged natures have been broken down, then in words of warm affection revealing emotions which may have been sealed through a lifetime. He said few words; these words could scarce have been fewer. It is true that a difficult commandment for a religious person to keep is the fifth, and that often for the sake of Christ, bonds of affection have to be broken. Family life and traditions have to be interrupted for the gospel's sake; but none had so completely to break with old ties as Christ. He had to do the will of His Father in heaven. The natural relationship vanished, and only the spiritual relationship could endure. But His mother's ministrations He could not have forgotten, and He shows this by commending her to the disciple He loved. Still, are we wrong in fancying that she must have craved for some more unrestrained expression of affection to live on when He was gone? If so, it was denied, and in that very denial we have an instructive proof that He who hung upon the Cross was more than man.[1]

4. We have seen how our Lord came gradually nearer to Himself, beginning with His enemies, then coming to one now His friend, then to His mother. He speaks now not to any of the people, but to God.

[1] I make these remarks with considerable diffidence, as an opposite view has, so far as I know, been universally taken. But one of our greatest poets makes a dying son say "Father" over and over again on his deathbed, because he wished "to gather up his sonship before he departed." Jesus says "Father"; He does not say "Mother."

A deep darkness came over the land, in the midst of which He remained silent, till at last He said, "My God! my God! why hast thou forsaken me?" It was dark, because the Light of the world was going out, and there was darkness also in the Saviour's soul. This was the crucifixion of His heart. He felt shut out from the presence, from the face of God. "Why hast thou forsaken me?" We cannot pretend to understand the meaning of this great darkness that enshrouded the Saviour's spirit, but we may point out that He still remained the Son. Yet, not "My Father," He says, but "My God." Still it is "*My* God, *my* God." There is no wavering, no distrust. He was not actually lost, neither did God's wrath rest upon Him for His own sin; it was "*My* God, *my* God." The clasp tightens in the dark. The record of the word is an instance of fearless candour. "That voice of utter loneliness in the death struggle is entirely credible," says one, "because it never could have been invented."

We cannot give a reply to this question other than the blessed old answer of the Scripture: "He was wounded for our transgressions, and bruised for our iniquities, the chastisement of our peace was upon Him." As with Gethsemane, the attempt to explain the agony by merely natural causes is palpably inadequate. Not the pain of His body, not the desertion of His friends, could have wrapped Him in darkness so deep and black. Our weighty sins which He bare in His own body on the tree made Him very heavy. And because of this His suffering escaped Him in this thrilling cry: "My God, my God, why hast thou forsaken me?"

5. Having uttered to God the complaint of His soul, He now utters the complaint of His body: "I thirst." The tide of His grief had reached its limit, and began to be assuaged. He was now able to note the sufferings of His body. It was eighteen or twenty hours since He had tasted anything. He had hung six hours on the Cross. Note the simple manliness of the utterance. He thirsted, and He was not ashamed to confess it. An Indian brave, ringed in with fire, would refuse to let a cry escape his black and swollen lips; but the Saviour of the world makes known His agony—"I thirst." He condescended to ask a draught, though He was on the very steps of the throne.

"I thirst." If He had chosen, He might have made the land alive with the ripple of sweet water. He created all wells and streams, and yet He thirsted with a bitter, burning, raging thirst. As He had thirsted before by the well, so now, but far more intensely, He thirsted again, and there was none found to help. The hour of thirst was an hour of danger. The adversary plied Him with the old temptation. He was tempted to say, "I will command these waters to quench my thirst," but He refuses. He was to see to the bottom of this mystery, and to drink the cup to the dregs, and to lay before His Father a will that had never swerved.

"I thirst—not for water only, but for rest, for home, for the end of all this." With desire He desired to eat and drink in the house of His Father. But the cup was almost drained, and He opened His lips next in the words—

6. "It is finished." There was still a little time

before the soul of Jesus parted from the body which had long been its troublous framework; but the agony was over, and the exulting sense of triumph and reward had come in. He had finished the work that God gave Him to do. Nothing had been left undone or unendured, and so He looks back on all the past, and says, "It is finished."

The meaning of the pronoun we do not attempt to expound in its whole blessed import. We take it simply as referring to the work which God had given Him to do. When we read it, we feel instantly how great a distance there is between Christ's life and ours. None ever spoke in that way. Our life is full of ragged edges, of incompleted tasks. Dying, we long for a little time to fulfil our dear dreams; but it is not given. "My book, my book," were the last words of a well-known writer on his forlorn deathbed; and all of us, when it comes to the end, will long for a little season more in which to put the finishing touch to something, that we may leave some completed work behind us. But we must die and leave things unfinished. He did all things well,—at the right time, in the right place, in the right way, neither too much nor too little. "It is finished"—it was done, and He could rest.

"It is finished." The great sacrifice for the sins of the whole world was offered. We who have broken God's law, and finished nothing, have a new and living way made open by His blood. When He said, "It is finished," His joy was not for Himself, merely that His suffering was over, but for His people—that the poorest, and the most sinful, and the most imperfect, might now come in all peace to God—that a door had been opened which no man and no demon could shut.

From His earliest years He had been busy in the things of His Father. His lifelong sustenance had been to do the will of Him that sent Him, and to finish His work; and now that the work is finished, the confidence of faith utters itself in the joyous cry—

7. "Father, into thy hands I commend my spirit." We who cannot say "It is finished," are fain to add to these words, "For thou hast redeemed me, Lord God of truth." "I go," said one of old, entering a monastery; "I go to a logic that fears not the logic of death." That logic is, "Father, into thy hands I commend my spirit, *for* thou hast redeemed me." Not till our sinful souls are cleansed and redeemed can we commit them to the holy hands of the Father; but He who could say "It is finished," committed a perfectly white soul to God. He needed not to speak of redemption. He had fulfilled the law, and so the soul that had done and borne all He committed into the sure unwearied hands of His Father. It was a most blessed thing to fall into those hands, and so He cries with a loud voice, "Father, into thy hands I commend my spirit."

"It is a fearful thing to fall into the hands of the living God." It is a fearful thing to have to part reluctantly from life, to be dragged out of it with sin cleaving to the soul. It is a fearful thing to fall into the hands of the tremendous energy of life and righteousness, without being prepared for the meeting. But it is a blessed thing to yield oneself in peaceful trust, knowing that one has not to fall far, and the fall is into the hands of the living Father. But Jesus used these words as none other could. He deepened them, and with Him they mean: "I who do not, unless I choose, need to lose hold of life, of my own will and by my own act let it go. My soul is not required, but by my own choice I commend it, my Father, to thee. No man could take my life from me; I lay it down of myself." Without claiming for ourselves the whole profound meaning of these words, we may yet use them as expressing the habitual temper of our lives, and, supremely, our frame of mind at death. Not to a tyrant, not to an unknown force, but to the God and Father of our Lord Jesus Christ we belong, living and dying. "Trust in God," says Faber, "is the last of all things, and the whole of all things."

XX

THE BURIAL AND RESURRECTION OF CHRIST

"The Lord is risen indeed."

"One place alone had ceased to hold its prey,
    A form had pressed it, and was there no more;
The garments of the grave beside it lay,
    Where once they wrapped Him, on the rocky floor.

"He only with returning footsteps broke
    The eternal calm wherewith the tomb was bound;
Among the sleeping dead alone He woke,
    And blessed with outstretched hands the hosts around.

"Well is it that such blessing hovers here,
    To soothe each sad survivor of the throng,
Who haunt the portals of the solemn sphere,
    And pour their woe the loaded air along."

IX. Poems by V.

CHAPTER XX

THE BURIAL AND RESURRECTION OF CHRIST

IT is part of Paul's gospel that Christ was buried, and there are circumstances of peculiar significance connected with the burial. His body after death was not dishonoured as others were. Instead of being left to hang on the cross to be profaned by the soldiers, it was taken down and laid by loving hands most reverently in the tomb. With that strange consonance which marks all the history, He who was born of a virgin was laid in a virgin grave. He was as a wayfaring man that turned aside to tarry for a night, and He was well lodged in that dark inn. His grave was in a garden, amidst the springing flowers, beneath the soft Syrian sunshine: there the Rose of Sharon was laid amongst the roses. There is here a prophecy, whether designed or not. Just as the flowers in winter weather go down into their roots, and keep house there till the breath of spring summons them, so He lay down for the appointed time to rise again.

He saw, it is written, no corruption. The stone which covered Him was more changed than He. Everything in the world which His spirit had left was changed save the body that lay sleeping in the holy grave. There He lay, with the flowers around

Him, wrapped in fine linen, waiting for the summons. Yet it is to be noticed also that this tomb was a borrowed tomb. He had died for our sakes poor, and so, though the grave allotted Him was the best that love could give, it was still a borrowed grave. We mark also the condition of the grave when He left it. The napkin about His head was not lying with the linen clothes, but wrapt together in a place by itself. All His life through, in every point, He had fulfilled the will of God; and so it was fit, when He arose from the dead, that He should keep the fair order still. The napkin was laid by itself. Every violation of order, if not a sin, is yet something akin to sin. Although it is hard to keep order in a world where all things are gone awry, yet in the life of Christ everything was done in perfect order, as we saw even in the cry which He uttered in the agony of His death. We see here also the calmness with which, unflushed by His risen power, He begins His work. In no flutter or perturbation He uses the resurrection power put into His hands.

He rose again from the dead. That is the central affirmation of the Christian faith. If this falls, all the rest falls; if this stands, all the rest will stand. This may excuse us if we depart a little from the plan of this book, and consider briefly the proof of the Resurrection, before we look at the bearings of the Resurrection on the work of Christ, and on our individual lives.

The proof of the Resurrection is the living Church of Jesus Christ. The life of the Church proves the life of the Saviour. When Jesus Christ died, His disciples, as might be expected, were plunged in profound despair. When the Shepherd was smitten, the flock was scattered abroad. But no long time had passed before a great revolution took place. They were at first in despair, in spite of all that He had said. His enemies were quicker to discern the meaning of His prophecies than His disciples, and their fears were stronger than His disciples' hopes. No collapse could be imagined more complete than that which took place at the entombment of the Saviour; but in a little time all was changed. The men who before had been cowards, slow of heart to believe, were completely transformed. They became brave and strong, and full of the most resolved faith. It was not that their outward circumstances had changed. They were sheep in the midst of wolves, and the beginning of their conflict with the world might have been expected to disappoint rather than encourage them; but instead of that, they have a new faith in the power of Jesus Christ—a faith which transforms them and makes them men. What explains this? Something must have happened in the interval to account for so marvellous a transformation. Nothing can explain it, save the Resurrection of Jesus Christ. That Resurrection breathed into them new faith, and hope, and strength, by virtue of which they faced fearlessly the most formidable odds, and most determined enemies. That is the explanation of Paul. It has never been denied, even by the extremest scepticism, that the First Epistle to the Corinthians was written within thirty-five years after the death of Christ. In that Epistle the whole gospel is built on the risen Christ. Jesus had broken the fetters of the tomb—the Lord had risen indeed; and in the strength of that risen Lord His disciples were henceforth to fight.

The truth of this explanation appears more clearly when we consider the utter inadequacy of all others. The old theory was that the disciples and Christ had conspired to deceive; but that is so impossible that it must be said to be entirely surrendered. The dullest must perceive that an institution like the Church of Christ cannot be built upon deceit. Deceit so enormous, so heartless, does not produce such fruit as this. And now the explanation given is that they were not deceivers, but themselves deceived. Had there been a want of witnesses, had the witnesses been few, had the facts to be explained been less numerous and less significant, it might have been possible to conceive of such an explanation; but that all should be befooled, that all should go harmoniously and unalterably mad, that such a faith as theirs,—a faith which shrank from no sacrifice, even from the sacrifice of life itself,—that such a faith should come out of an imposture, is utterly incredible. A sentence may serve to dismiss the mythical theory. Events were too quick for the slow growth of myths. No forcing frame could have produced such results so speedily. So we can rest on the truth that the Lord is risen indeed; and in that we find the only possible solution—a risen Christ. Faith in the risen Christ has made the Church what it is to-day.[1]

---

[1] To say that the evidence for the Resurrection resolves itself into an undefined belief on the part of a few persons, in a

BURIAL AND RESURRECTION OF CHRIST

We now look at the bearings of the Resurrection on the work of Christ. The Resurrection is no mere supplement to the work of Christ, but an integral and essential part. He Himself always coupled the two things: "The Son of man must go to Jerusalem, and suffer many things of the elders and chief priests and scribes, and be killed, and be raised again the third day." Though the light of the message of the Resurrection was lost in the gloom of the announcement of His death, as it fell first on the startled ears of the disciples, we are able to see that death was not the end, but the centre of His work. Death, it is true, as we have seen, was in a sense a vital part of His work, but death had always to be thought of along with Resurrection. He appealed to the Resurrection as the final test of His work. "Destroy this temple," He said, speaking of the temple of His body, "and I will raise it up in three days." In other words, He claimed not merely that He would rise, but that He would raise Himself. Again, He told His disciples that the Spirit would convince the world of righteousness, because He went to the Father. In other words—If He did not go to the Father, if He continued to lie amongst the dead, His whole work was a failure, and He Himself a deceiver of the people. If He really saw corruption, and became subject to death as others do, the trust which

notoriously superstitious age, that after Jesus had died and been buried they had seen Him alive (*Supernatural Religion*, iii. 522), is to mistake the facts. The faith revolutionised expectation, changed character, and expressed itself in the most vivid symbols.

He claims in life and in death cannot be given Him. There may be a question as to what would be left even then in His life and teaching for man to prize, but there is no need that we should enter into the mournful inquiry as to how much might be saved out of so disastrous a ruin. If He was really God, He must rise. If He be holden of death, and if His dust sleeps to-day beneath the Syrian skies, then out of His own mouth we condemn Him, and His own words give us warrant for believing that His work of redemption is no redemption at all. But if, instead of that, we see the great stone rolled away, if we find the grave empty, if we meet Him as He was when He lay down, with no touch of corruption or trace of death, hailing Him in that newness of life, we see that the Father has set His seal upon His work, and accepted it, and that His claims to be righteous are verified by the voice from heaven. So we go to the grave and look into its emptiness, and listen to the angel message, "He is not here; He is risen," and see the light of hope and joy passing through the hearts of the disciples, and we are convinced of righteousness. All that is deepest in His own words, all that is greatest in His works, is utterly lost unless He be risen. But, having risen, He is declared to be the Son of God by that divine voice which aforetime had proclaimed Him to be the beloved Son—the voice heard at His baptism, at His transfiguration, and before His death. That voice, clearer than ever, says, when He rises from the grave, and sets death beneath His feet, "This is my beloved Son, hear ye Him." But not only is the Resurrection an attestation of His work, but it signifies that His death is not the end of His work, but its centre. In one sense His work was finished when He died, but in another sense it was only carried into its centre, that it might be completed in heaven. With all men besides, death is the end of work for this world. The work of Moses, for example, was before his death, and we remember him, not for his death, nor for his work in heaven, but on account of his long, faithful, and patient labour before he died. And so, when men die, and their work is over, their influence begins to decrease. Others take up and carry on the new work of the world, and these are remembered and honoured. But the centre of the work of Christ was His death, and his death was not the completion of His work. His work is carried on in heaven at the right hand of God, and this is why His name must grow. The servants decrease; they have their day, and cease to be. They are broken lights of God, and are caught up one by one into the great splendour. But the name of Christ grows brighter and greater continually; for although He called us by His death from the death of trespasses and sins, and although He made it possible for guilty men to be reconciled to God, He has done nothing for us that is really enduring unless He be risen to give us power to walk in newness of life. If we have been called from death simply to fall back again into death, we have been mocked by a transient gleam, which left the darkness deeper than it found it. But He calls us to newness of life, and it is by His power working in heaven that we are guided in that risen life, and enabled, in spite of the world, the flesh, and the devil, to retain it. He was declared to be the Son of God with power, and that power He is using in the upper realm for the extension of His Church, and for the upbuilding of His people.

Leaving this point to be touched upon more fully when we come to speak of the Ascension, we pass on to note the bearing of the Resurrection of Christ on our own resurrection. If Christ be not risen, there is nothing to preach and nothing to believe. If Christ is not risen, there is no future life; and if there is no future life, our faith is vain and our preaching is vain. We are, as the great apostle said, of all men most miserable. The gospel is the gospel of the Resurrection as much as it is the gospel of the death of Christ. Is it then true that the Resurrection certifies to us a future life? We have to face, every one of us, the last enemy, death. Ever since the world began, all who have entered it sooner or later have had this struggle, and the battle has always ended in one way. Two indeed escaped, but they did not escape by meeting and mastering their foe — they escaped by being taken away before the battle. We all know that we shall soon meet with this great combatant. We shall use in the struggle every resource that the experience of the centuries has suggested. All that love can do, all that skill and science can do, all the power of tears and prayers, will be tried, and yet the result is sure: we must yield, he must be the conqueror. It is true that advancing knowledge has probably prolonged for a little the life of man; yet even against that little gain must be set the fact that death is often more painful when life is continued in conditions where of old it could not be maintained. Nor is this all. Not only does death take all captive, but all whom he has taken he appears, so far as we can see, to keep. Every victory that he has gained he is able to retain. The turf lies unbroken over those whom we laid beneath it, and no device of man has been able to take from death what he has conquered. There are hours when we feel, even to anguish and despair, the terror of the unbroken victory of death. Almost every other struggle has its ebbs and flows—backward and forward rolls the tide of battle. Hopes that were like to die are suddenly and wondrously revived; but in this great battle of death there is one result, and only one.

What are we to say in the presence of this mystery? What did the people of God stay their hearts upon before the coming of Christ? In reply we do not think it can be questioned that in their highest moments of faith and hope they saw that the man created in God's image, and living in God's love, must live again.[1] "If a man die," said Job, "shall he live again?" And he answered his own question after a fashion. "As for me," said another in a great ecstasy of faith, "I shall behold thy face in righteousness; I shall be satisfied when I wake with thy likeness." Job looked forward to the time when he would rise. Many days might intervene before the summons came from heaven, "but all the days of my

[1] See Note E.

appointed time will I wait till my change come. All the time between I will count nothing, if I only know that I shall not be left for ever; and I know that the divine heart in its own time will move towards me. 'Thou shalt call, and I will answer— thou shalt have a desire to the work of thine own hands.'" In other words: "Thou hast made me, soul and body, fearfully and wonderfully, with those longings for immortality and thee; and the time will come when thou wilt have need of me, and call me from my slumber." That is the great achievement of faith, and the very greatness of that faith made it brief and rare. In supreme moments of vision and power the Old Testament saints were enabled so to believe and so to speak, but for the most part they had to move on a lower level; for their faith, though founded on a true conception of themselves and of God, was not able to build upon any explicit promise, far less upon any divine fact; and so, when hours of darkness came, and the onward sweep of the victory of death was unbroken, they sank down again. Only a great hope in God could make them believe surely in the resurrection life.

"If a man die, shall he live again?" Job's question has been re-echoed by many a broken heart not able to echo his victorious answer. Many centuries passed before it was answered by Jesus. But the answer when it came was complete and clear. "I am the Resurrection and the Life," saith the Lord: "he that believeth in me, though he were dead, yet shall he live; and he that believeth in me shall never die." Upon this strong assurance we can now fall back. We have gone to the grave with our dear ones, and have seen the dust fall on the coffin lid, and have asked whether the gate which we have closed in our sorrow shall ever be opened again, and we have been able to answer in these words of Christ. But the mere assurance of words is not enough. It is beautiful, and strong, and comforting; but we need something more; we need to know that one has actually faced the dread combatant and mastered him; that he has plucked the sting from death, and spoiled the victory of the grave. And it is only when we know and are sure that He who said these words has verified them by His own victory, that the fearful questioning of death and the grave receive an answer which can satisfy. Jesus Christ rose from the dead, and became the first-fruits of His sleeping people. He overcame the sharpness of death, and rose and revived; and because He lives, we shall live also. This thought of Christ's conquest for us over death may be broken into two parts:—There is first the continued life of the soul. If we are united to Christ by faith, a life streams into our souls, which the grave cannot touch, far less destroy. "He that believeth in me shall not die." Death to such a life is but a passing gloom, soon lost in the sunshine. It is not able to interrupt, far less finally to break, the tie that binds to Christ. As a river runs through a lake, and pursues its crystal way beyond, not lost by its passing through the intervening waters, so the life given through faith that is in Jesus Christ flows on through the marshes and the swamps of death, and comes out clear at the other side. Not only so.

The fact that the essential life remains, guarantees that by and by all else that is worth saving will be saved. That is the meaning and the proof of the resurrection of the body. Jesus Christ died to redeem the soul in the first instance, but He also died to redeem the body. And though we have to wait long for the redemption of the body, and though death does his dishonouring work, yet He who has put His hand to the work will finally complete it, and, having brought the soul to Himself, He will by and by bring its companion also. Dearer than the dust of Zion to the ancient saints is the dust of His redeemed people to the Lord Jesus; and though it may be driven and scattered by the winds of centuries, it shall be re-gathered, and all that is really precious, all that is really part of ourselves, shall live. We can say to death, "Thou hast no power at all over my soul, and thou couldst have none over my body, except it were given thee from above." The perfect man shall be brought at last into the heaven where the glorified Man Christ Jesus sits enthroned.

> "The swallow leaves her nest,
> The soul my weary breast,
> But therefore let the rain
>   On my grave
> Fall pure; for why complain,
> Since both will come again
>   O'er the wave?"[1]

It is impossible, then, to over-estimate the importance of the fact of the Resurrection. If this miracle is credible, all the rest are credible. If Jesus

[1] T. L. Beddoes.

be risen from the dead, He was and still remains the Son of God with power; if He be risen from the dead, then, in spite of all appearances, death is not conqueror but conquered; if He be risen from the dead, then the souls of believers are at their death made perfect in holiness, and do immediately pass into glory, while their bodies, being still united to Christ, do rest in their graves until the resurrection. But no longer; for they then rise in the likeness of His glorious body, and the long-parted companions are joined together, and so are ever with the Lord.

XXI
THE RESURRECTION LIFE OF CHRIST

"Touch me not, for I am not yet ascended."

"We were not by when Jesus came,
    But round us far and near
We see His trophies, and His name
    In choral echoes hear.
In a fair ground our lot is cast,
As in the solemn week that past,
While some might doubt, but all adored,
Ere the whole widowed Church had seen her Risen Lord."

KEBLE.

CHAPTER XXI

THE RESURRECTION LIFE OF CHRIST

THE great truth signified by Christ's Resurrection, that death to those who believe in Him is not an interruption, but an intensifying of life, not a separation from God, but an entrance into the immediate presence of the Father of spirits, has been already dwelt on. But the significance of the fact is by no means exhausted by this truth. Other raisings from the dead recorded in the Bible were restorations to the old conditions of earthly life; the Resurrection of Christ was the revelation of a new life. The daughter of Jairus, the young man at Nain, and Lazarus, resumed their places, and were to their friends what they had been. Jesus re-entered the world under new and glorious conditions.

During the forty days in which He was on earth, He appeared at least eleven times. Of these appearances, nine are recorded in the Gospels. The first appearance was to Mary Magdalene in the garden. Out of her seven devils had been cast, and we find her, along with the other women who crossed the illuminated track, and are still visible, following the

Lord, and ministering to Him of her substance. She was last at the cross, and when all was over came to the tomb with spices to anoint Him. Returning in the dusk of the morning, she found the grave empty, and ran for the rest. Jesus spoke to her, calling her by name, "Mary." She did not know Him at first, but supposed Him to be the gardener, and asked where the dead body of her Lord had been taken, offering, weak woman though she was, to take it away herself. She then recognised Him, exclaimed "Rabboni," and moved as if to clasp His feet. He gently, but decisively, repelled her: "Touch me not, for I am not yet ascended to my Father, and to your Father; to my God, and your God." He refused to be touched, not because He was unclean, nor because His new dignity repelled advance, but simply because her gesture and her word, "My Master," showed that she was looking forward to the old relations being resumed, and not to the new and more glorious conditions that were to be established. "Touch me not, for I am not yet ascended. The time is coming when the old intimacy of affection, the old unbroken companionship, may be resumed; but that time is not yet. Still it is coming. This presence that you cannot have now, will be yours in the future. When I am ascended, you may cling to me. The spiritual clinging then hereafter, and the fact that my Father is your Father, and my God is your God, show that you and I will at last be together." Still it was a disappointment to her faithful love, and He gives her, of His rich mercy, a compensation, "Go, tell my brethren." She was

THE RESURRECTION LIFE OF CHRIST

thus made an apostle to the apostles of the fact that the Lord had risen.

He appeared next to Mary Magdalene and Joanna, who came together to see the sepulchre, when He commanded them to go and tell His brethren to go into Galilee, that there they should see Him. He thus imposed on the disciples a task of some difficulty, sending them to the northern province, partly for their own sakes, partly that the witnesses to His rising might be diffused, and the proof of His death made abundant, and partly, no doubt, because He wished to gaze again on the haunts of His childhood—His old home, the hills which He had climbed, the lake on which He had sailed, the faces on which He had looked. It was in obedience to a feeling, human, true, and manly, that He sought His childhood's home.

The third appearance was probably to Simon Peter alone; and the fourth was when He joined His disciples on the way to Emmaus. Two of them, who had nothing that we know of to draw His company, save their profound grief, were journeying together, talking of the wreck and ruin which had overtaken their hopes, when suddenly He joined Himself to their company. He asked what they were speaking of, and, on being told, opened up to them, in all the Scriptures, the things concerning Himself. God was walking with these ignorant men, though they knew it not, and as He talked their hearts burned within them. They come at last to the house, and He made as though He would go farther—a touch of true and refined human feeling; "the first true gentleman," says an old dramatist, "that ever breathed." He would not press Himself unasked upon their courtesy, nor even seem to do so. As if to relieve them of possible embarrassment, He made as though He would have gone farther, but they constrained Him, and He enters with them, and sits down to such poor fare as they were able to set before Him. The meal goes on, and in the course of it He takes and breaks the bread. Their eyes are opened, and they know Him, and He vanishes out of their sight. He had always been the head of the little family. Always when He is a guest He becomes the host, as at Cana, and now, and in the human soul, so long as His work of ingathering goes on. "If any man will open, I will enter in and sup with him, and he with me." What had not been discovered by His words, this simple act revealed—they knew Him. Possibly when He was handling the bread they saw the marks in His hands of what He had gone through, or more likely the way in which He handled the bread brought all to mind—"they knew Him." Often a little thing will bring back the thronged and eventful past. A stray odour may restore long vanished gardens and hands that have crumbled into dust, a bit of blue ribbon bring back a life we thought ourselves utterly done with, and repeople it with the old forms. So they knew Him, and instead of staying to enlighten them still farther with His company, He vanished out of their sight. They had work to do—to go to Jerusalem and tell the apostles; and so He departs.

He appears next to the ten disciples gathered together without Thomas. They were sitting with shut doors for fear of the Jews, when suddenly the thin air yielded His form. They were terrified and affrighted, supposing that they had seen a ghost. The strange dread of the spiritual world, which witnesses so impressively our sense of antagonism with it, took possession of them. He allayed their doubts by asking them to handle Him, and see that He was not a spirit, but His old self. They ought to have known Him. All His promises should not have been so soon forgotten. Yet He does not upbraid them, but seeks to satisfy their doubts. It would have been better that they should have known Him; and thus souls are happiest who from childhood unto death have offered Him the unbroken service of intellect and will. But such are few, and to others He will give all the proof that they can reasonably require.

These appearances occurred on the day of the Resurrection. The fifth appearance took place on the following Lord's-day, to the disciples assembled with Thomas. Thomas was a doubter, as we have seen, of a peculiar type. His love did not wander though his intellect was not satisfied. His faith was shown in act by his staying with the disciples. He had evidently a deep and vivid recollection of the gaping wounds. That death which he had anticipated when the Lord was to raise Lazarus had come, but in a worse form than his worst fears. Jesus offers him the fullest opportunity of testing Him. The disciple is broken down without availing himself of the proffer. He shows how great and deep a faith the scepticism of the intellect had for a moment paralysed, by saying, "My Lord and my God,"—an unreserved acknowledgment of the Saviour's divinity, and thus a great advance upon Mary's "My Master."

He appeared next to the disciples—five named—and others by the Sea of Galilee, where He held His touching conversation with Simon Peter. There had been the secret interview before, when the apostle was again united to His Redeemer. How eagerly this interview had been anticipated we may judge from the character of Peter, a man who could not have been content to rest in his denials, and whose agonies would have been intensified when the thought shot through him that he never would have an opportunity of gaining the pardon of the Master whom he had wronged. The outbursts of that great penitent heart, the loving correction of the Saviour—these are too sacred for outside observation, and accordingly this interview, though explicitly referred to, is not given in any of its details. But there had to be not only the union of the man to his Saviour, but the restoration of the apostle to his place, and this was solemnly done after a thrice repeated question, "Lovest thou me?" If he loved, all was well. He was able to appeal to omniscience: "Thou knowest all things; thou knowest that I love thee." The apparent contradiction was understood, and Peter was restored. What he was as an apostle after the Ascension we know. His patience under wrong, his calmness in controversy, his heroic martyrdom—these are proofs that he was not unworthy of the great charge thus solemnly recommitted to him.

He appeared again to the eleven on a mountain in Galilee; to five hundred brethren; to James His brother; and to the eleven at Jerusalem, before the Ascension; and last of all at the Ascension.

These appearances are characterised by a strange union of remoteness and clearness, depth and simplicity. The tomb where He was laid was found empty. He appeared and disappeared at pleasure. All that belonged to His humanity was preserved, and at the same time all was transfigured. A sceptic puts the following dilemma: "One or other alternative must be adopted—if Jesus possessed His own body after His Resurrection, and could eat and be handled, He could not vanish; if He vanished, He could not be corporeal." But the very point of the revelation is that these two things are reconciled. Nothing is lost in the passage through death, and yet the limitations of the present order of things are not perpetuated.

1. As regards His body, we are taught that the crucified body and the glorified body are connected. The wounds are there—these at least are common to the two. Thus it is signified that through all eternity He is a man, that in heaven the marks of His death speak and plead, and that the future judgment of His people is the judgment of their Redeemer.

Along with this it is taught that the spiritual body is not trammelled as the physical body is. He has entered upon a new state. At the very time when He offers a material test of the reality of His presence, He shows that He is not bound by the laws of matter. In His life He very rarely departed from the ordinary ways of motion, but after His Resurrection He moves from place to place without any apparent passage. He is seen within shut doors; He eats, but does not seem to have need of food. This proves the possibility of a spiritual body that shall be recognisable—a body which we shall know and in which we shall be known, and at the same time a body in which we shall not be burdened —in which the outer frame will be a help and not a hindrance to the spirit within.

2. Besides this, these appearances are instructive as showing the abiding laws which govern the manifestation of the Lord Jesus to His disciples. The Resurrection was the beginning of a new and living relation between the Lord and His people. The Lord who was raised lives and manifests Himself to His disciples. They needed, in the first place, to know that He was really risen; and they needed, in the next place, to understand that the old earthly relationships were gone. He weans them gradually from these, that He may prepare them for doing without them.

Such facts as these are illustrated. Jesus Christ, during the forty days, did not manifest Himself to or communicate in any way with those outside of the Church. His visits were exclusively to His disciples. The continuity of His risen life may be seen from this— "If a man love me, I will manifest myself to him." Again, the manifestations are given to those who are in special need, and are carefully adapted to supply that need. To Peter, when the two were alone, and in the presence of the rest; to Mary, and to Thomas, He manifests Himself. Tenderness and reproof are mingled. There is a remarkable individuality in each interview, but the issue of each is the same—the communication of new strength and faith. Again, He manifests Himself sometimes to one, sometimes to two or three, more frequently to all assembled together; and the promise still holds: "Where two or three are gathered together in my name, there am I in the midst of them." "If two of you shall agree as touching anything ye shall ask, it shall be done for you by my Father which is in heaven." Once more, it is manifest that in all, Christ Himself, independent of other things, is the all-sufficient happiness of His children.

So then, just as before His crucifixion He gives us a prayer that helps us to understand His eternal intercession, so now we have in these forty days pregnant instances of the precise way in which He is to be present with His people for their comfort and refreshment even unto the end.

I need not say much of the divine originality of this idea. The combination of truth between one-sided Materialism and one-sided Spiritualism, a conception for which the apostles had absolutely no precedent, and which even yet men find a most difficult and strange idea, cannot be explained on any other supposition than the facts. Strange and difficult though the idea may be, it is nevertheless the only one that will harmonise the apparently antithetic experiences of our perplexing life.[1]

[1] See Note F.

XXII
THE ASCENSION OF CHRIST

"Thou hast ascended on high."

"If Christ was only six hours crucified,
After few years of toil and misery,
Which for mankind He suffered willingly,
While heaven was won for ever when He died;—
Why should He still be shown on every side,
Painted and preached, in nought but agony,
Whose pains were light matched with His victory,
When the world's power to harm Him was defied?
Why rather speak and write not of the realm
He rules in heaven, and soon will bring below,
Unto the praise and glory of His name?
Ah, foolish crowd! The world's thick vapours whelm
Your eyes, unworthy of that glorious show,
Blind to His splendour, bent upon His shame."
MICHAEL ANGELO.

CHAPTER XXII

THE ASCENSION OF CHRIST

WE have seen how Christ entered the world, how He bore Himself in it, how He died and rose again from the grave. How is He to leave the world in a manner that shall harmonise with His entrance into it and His life there? There is, there can be, but one answer — He ascended. Not much about the Ascension is said in Scripture, and in lives of Christ it is often dismissed in a few brief lines; many large and important truths, however, are wrapt up in the story. He was not the first to go into the other world by another gate than that of death. Enoch was translated that he should not see death, and a chariot of fire was sent to take Elijah home. But these translations, instead of resembling the Ascension of Christ, rather show His divinity by their contrast with it.

Jesus Christ ascended by His own power and His own will. "I go to my Father" — "I leave the world and go to my Father." There was no doubt the power of the Father working along with that of the Son. "After He had blessed them, He was parted from them, and carried up into heaven." Still the primary idea is that He ascended. How sharply this separates Him from Enoch and Elijah! Enoch, we are told, walked quietly with God, and one day he was lifted gently by the divine Hand out of the turbulences of sin that were round about him. He did not ascend himself; God took him. Then, Elijah was taken up to heaven by a whirlwind. He did not fix the time or the way of his departure. But God knew when his work was done, and when His purpose had been wrought to its last refinement, He removed him. He sent for him a fiery chariot. As He appointed the time, so He made the way. In fit keeping with Elijah's fiery and impetuous life was his departure in the chariot and horses that took him up the track of flame to his home with God. It has been strikingly suggested that the very force and violence of the translation show the difficulty with which mortal flesh can be taken into heaven. There was a great and manifest expenditure of power in bearing the prophet up, but nothing can be more easy and tranquil than the Ascension of Christ. As His life was gentle and His death calm, so without noise or ostentation He rose up to His glory. He was parted from them and carried up into heaven. They watched Him ascending, and they might have seen His shadow on the sward as He bore His way upward, until at last a cloud received Him out of their sight. As He was God, it was more natural for Him to ascend into heaven than it was for Him to come down to earth. Descent is natural and only too easy to man. It is for God to ascend; and so, in obedience to His own will, and in accordance with the laws of His own nature, He rose out of their sight into heaven. He ascended.

Again, Jesus Christ differed from all the rest in leaving behind Him a finished work. He had died for the sin of the world, and His offering was so complete that nothing could be added to it. God alone finishes, man never can. "Our best finishing is but coarse and blundering work after all. We may smooth, and soften, and sharpen till we are sick at heart, but take a good magnifying-glass to our miracle of skill, and the invisible edge is a jagged saw, and the silky thread a rugged cable, and the soft surface a granite desert. Let all the ingenuity and all the art of the human race be brought to bear upon the attainment of the utmost possible finish, and they could not do what is done in the foot of a fly or the film of a bubble. God alone can finish, and the more intelligent the human mind becomes, the more the infiniteness of interval is felt between human and divine work in this respect."[1] Elijah left work which would be carried on after he was gone. Before he departed he went round to the three colleges of the prophets, and looked for the last time on the young men, then studying the scrolls of Israel, who were to succeed him. And so it is with all of us. We die, leaving our work to others, and the great teacher says to some beloved disciple, "You will take the banner I have been carrying for so many years, and bear it on to victory over my grave. You will take the message for which I have all my life been seeking to win an entrance, and speak it more powerfully and more tunefully, that the world may take from you what it never took from me." So Elijah hands on his work to Elisha—one prophet to another; and thus, though

[1] Ruskin.

the worker dies, the work goes on through the years of history. But Christ's work once accomplished was done for ever. Had He even failed to utter the words "I thirst," there would have been something incomplete, for it is profoundly said that He spoke thus in order that the Scriptures might be fulfilled. But no work had been left undone, no word unuttered, of all that He should do and say. So, while His apostles had successors, He had none, but stands by Himself.

But while in one sense His work was finished, in another it was carried on when He ascended. The work in heaven, although distinct from the work on earth, is nevertheless of one piece with it, and serves to accomplish the same great end. This at once marks Him off from every other benefactor of the race. Others say, "What shall I do for thee *before* I be taken from thee? While I live my life is thine—thine even to the last breath, the breath which may be spent in blessing you; but after I am taken from thee, my power is ended." Father and mother leave their children young and defenceless, and die, and the bitterness of death is that they can do nothing after it for those who are left behind. But Jesus within the veil carries on to completion the work which He began in the outer world. The veil is lifted in various parts of the New Testament, and especially in the Epistle to the Hebrews. And it is well to look at it, for although we can never think too often or too much about the Cross, we may think too little about the Throne. The finished work on which our faith reposes should not be dissevered from the work which is continually going on. Had He not taken His life up again for us, it would have been of no avail that He laid it down. He would have been only the victim of an enormous wrong; and it is because that He was not the victim, but the priest, that He works out a complete redemption. In heaven He is interceding for us. His prayers rise like a fountain for us through the endless day. Our intercessions rise and pause, His go on. Words can but remotely approximate to the truth here, but we are perhaps nearest when we say that His intercession is the perpetual presentation of His sacrifice and its claims before His Father.

Again, He is preparing a place for us. "In my Father's house," He said to the bewildered disciples that nestled near Him when the storm was darkening, "are many mansions; if it were not so, I would have told you. I have not hesitated rudely to dash your hopes hitherto when you needed it, and I would not have hesitated now; but a place in these mansions will be yours. I go to prepare it for you." Here again we touch things that can be but dimly understood. We may, indeed, conjecture this—God through many thousands of years prepared for man his home during the brief day of time, so it is not unworthy that through mighty periods He should continue the preparation of the endless resting-place of His children. But whether this be so or not, the presence of the glorified humanity of Jesus Christ seems a necessary condition and preliminary of our presence in heaven. We could not be at home amidst those august and terrible splendours unless we saw Him, our brother, in the heart of all. As Joseph's brethren, who had been all their lives wild Arab shepherds, would have felt ill at ease indeed in the proudest court of the world, had it not been that their brother was there upon the throne, so we would not have found heaven to be our home unless we found it to be the place of the presence of Jesus Christ. Heaven is no place for us unless Jesus Christ be there; and when we begin to shape our thoughts of heaven into a whole, we are soon arrested by incongruities and perplexities; but one thought we do not need to reject, one thought we repose in, that Christ is heaven, and heaven is He.

> "My knowledge of that life is small,
>   The eye of faith is dim;
> But 'tis enough that Christ knows all,
>   And I shall be with Him."

"To depart is to be with Christ." The simplicity of the one thought is far better than a host of distracting and disturbing conceptions.

It is the presence of Christ that will secure our bliss in heaven, even as it secures our entrance. The angels fell by their own transgression from the habitation of light to the nethermost gloom; and if we are saved, it is not because we are holier or stronger, but because we have been united to Christ as the angels never were. Our union to Him brings us through the thorny mazes of life to rest, and our union keeps us in the rest. Where Christ is, we are; and were it possible that Christ should leave heaven, we, His people, would follow Him.

Elisha never asked from Elijah that he would use for him his influence in the courts above. He never said, "When you reach heaven, pray for me";

never asked him to look down upon his work and to help it on, but, "Let me have now, before you depart, something that will help me for the time I linger here." One martyr, it is true, said to another, "So long as I understand thou art on thy journey, by God's grace I shall call upon our heavenly Father, for Christ's sake, to let thee safely home; and then, good brother, speak thou and pray for the remnant which are to suffer for Christ's sake, according to that thou shalt then know more clearly."[1] But these are vague aspirations, hopes, conjectures. How different from the clear and well-grounded certainty of Christ's continual work for us!

Further, there is, corresponding to this, the thought that Jesus Christ still works in the world. Though He ascended, yet He descended again, and is in the heart of the fight, battling along with His soldiers, and leading them on to victory. Not merely does He think of them away in heaven, working within the veil, but says, "Lo, I am with you alway, even to the end of the world." Enthroned as He is in heaven at the right hand of God, He is not absent from the conflict that never pauses here. We have a wonderful picture of the Lord lifted up in heaven, and at the same time working on earth with His disciples, and giving them the victory. He sat down on the right hand of God, and the disciples went out everywhere preaching the word. Did He then rest and leave them to fight? Nay; the Lord was working with them, and confirming the word by signs

[1] Bishop Ridley to Bradford the martyr.

following. Not only does He work with the Church, but He works with the individual members. He helps us in our own special battle, in our own special burden. If faith is almost dying in any soul, because of the weight of grief, He will roll the stone away and let in the light. If corruption and temptation are too much for any soul, He will succour it ere it be overborne. If the little company of the militant Church are tempted to give up the battle in the face of the great hosts of evil, He, like those mysterious horsemen who succoured the Romans when the fight grew desperate, will interpose and turn the tide of battle. He served in the ranks before He became Commander, and He knows the difficulty of every soldier, whatever it may be. Especially is He with us by the gift of His Spirit. No departing leader could give his spirit except Christ. Elisha asked Elijah, "Let a double portion of thy spirit be upon me." The answer was, "Thou hast asked a hard thing." It was to ask for Elijah twice over, as if God would allow him to depart to heaven and leave the twofold energy of his life working behind him. "Thou hast asked a hard thing. It may be, it may not be, I cannot tell—if God wills it. And the sign will be, if thou see me when I am taken from thee, it shall be so unto thee; but if not, it shall not be so; the gift belongs to God." So, many a dying leader prays that his spirit may descend upon others, but he cannot pour out his spirit. Christ differs from all others in being able and willing to give His Spirit.

It is this chiefly which makes the name of Christ

so mighty in the world. All other names decrease; His increases still. We worship the rising sun, and it is the fate of all men gradually to fade. Their places are taken and their work is done by others, and their memory grows with the years more shadowed and less frequent. It is true that their work may be a permanent and recognisable force; but the years gradually separate from the worker, and while the influence of the one remains, the personality of the other grows more and more dim. There is something pathetic in the ineffectual centenaries and celebrations with which men struggle to keep alive a great name. But the years that rob other names of their brightness, only give new lustre to the name of Christ. His name endures and shines like the sun, because His work is continual. We feel the effects of the work of men who are dead, but there are no fresh discharges from the old centre of force, and so the memory of the worker is merged in his work; but the influence of Christ on the history of the race is permanently and steadily exercised, and this it is that makes His personality more fresh and vivid than that of any who are living and working with us still.

The Ascension of Christ marks for us the way to heaven. A track of light goes through the darkness into the heart of heaven. As He rose, so we shall rise. The ascension of Elijah left the way no clearer for Elisha. He went with him from Gilgal to Bethel, to Jericho, and to Jordan, but he could go no farther. What the next stage of the journey was, he must die to know. The mystery of death was as dark as ever. The transient light soon vanished, and was forgotten; but the Ascension of Christ is the pledge that the soul shall ascend. When the last breath is drawn, and the face settles into rest, we know that though the shell grows cold in death beside us, the soul has ascended, and is as distant as a thousand years. By the road which Christ took when He went out of the world unto the Father, do His people pass into Paradise.

He ascended, but He will come again. The Jews looked for the return of Elias before the great and notable day of the Lord, and perhaps the prophecy has not been completely fulfilled. But we do not look for the return of Elias. It is true that the saints are to come again — He will come with the saints and with His holy angels. When He comes, the righteous shall blaze out like the sun in the kingdom of the Father. "Them which sleep in Jesus will God bring with Him," and doubtless among the thronging legions each will find his own. But still that thought is nothing to the vast multitude—it is scarcely even a distinct conception, far less a ruling motive. How different with the coming of Christ! That is the hope of the Church. Still her eyes are turned eastward; and if she were not looking and hoping, faith and strength would fail. But He received the kingdom, and He went to rule that kingdom, and also to return; and although the years linger, and many doubt, and generation after generation passes away, we know that the heavens will break, the throne will be set, and the Lord will appear. Amen. Even so, come, Lord Jesus.

XXIII
THE CHARACTER OF CHRIST

"**Whosoever speaketh a word against the Son of man, it shall be forgiven him.**"

"By the light of burning martyr fires Christ's bleeding feet I track,
Toiling up new Calvaries ever, with the cross that turns not back."

J. R. LOWELL.

CHAPTER XXIII

THE CHARACTER OF CHRIST

"WHAT think ye of Christ?" What are we to say of His character? He belongs to the human race. Though born of a Jewish mother, He is claimed by all races as their own. What judgment must be passed of the universal Man? First, He was, according to His own claim, sinless. He tells us Himself that He was unimpeachable by Satan. Before men He could say, "Which of you convinceth me of sin?" He could go farther. Standing in the presence of His Father, He could say, "I do always the things that please thee." This claim men have never been able to refute. It is witnessed to by those who are friendly, by those who are indifferent, by those who are hostile,—by Judas, by Pilate, by the thief, by the centurion. But admit that the witness has come to us through partial statements, declare that the evangelists are untrustworthy, and still the fact faces us that they have carried out this faultless character into the details of life; and in the details of life, as in the processes of philosophy, error is likely to happen in descending. But these facts have been examined, and many attempts have been made to establish a charge of moral culpability against Jesus. The cursing of the fig-tree, the destruction of the swine, the expulsion of the traders, the harsh words to His mother at Cana, the alleged collision of duties between religious and political allegiance—these have been cited. It might be enough to reply that sin when present does not manifest itself in such homœopathic quantities as these. But, apart from that, careful examination has shown in each instance that the charges break down, that no soiling breath has been left upon the perfect clearness of the mirror. We reckon upon no forbearance from the enemy, and yet repeat again with perfect confidence His own challenge, "Which of you convinceth me of sin?" The voice of criticism dies away. It turns out that some fundamental circumstance has been overlooked, or some unwarranted assumption has been made; and so again, as at the first, there is silence.

Stronger even than this is His own witness of His sinlessness. Moral progress becomes more and more pervasive. Only a dull spiritual eye fails to see deficiency. The greatest and holiest servants of God all humble themselves before men and confess sin— "I am a man of unclean lips"; "O wretched man that I am!" The anthems in the Book of Psalms are strangely mixed with *misereres;* but we have long conversations and soliloquies of Christ, and we fail to find in them even one half sigh of penitence. He was not a Pharisee, for He was the scourger of Pharisees, the friend of publicans and sinners, and the lover of them who confessed their guilt. But He cannot take His place along with them. He lifts up His calm and trustful eyes to heaven, and says, "I have finished the work which thou gavest me to do." Even by the admission of Strauss, Jesus is in the department of religion what Shakespeare is in poetry and Alexander in war, and marks a limit which may be attained, but cannot be passed. In His sight the faintest speck would have been a fearful blot; but He knows of no blot. He cannot repent, however much He feels for them who need repentance. He feels sin, but does not do so as a sinner Himself, but as one who bears the guilt of sinners. What hopeless superiority to all missiles there is in the words, "Whosoever speaketh a word against the Son of man, *it shall be forgiven him!*" His claim to be the judge of men involves His sinlessness. That claim is absolute, not relative. He is ordinarily represented as having no assistance, and even the angels are only His attendants. Could the words, "Depart from me, ye cursed, into everlasting fire," come from the lips of one who had sinned? Besides, He claims to die for sinners. He is the Good Shepherd, who will lay down His life for the sheep. He will give His life a ransom for many, to procure the remission of their sins. How could such a statement be borne if He was not absolutely sinless? If He had ever been untruthful, vain, or cruel, what becomes of the atoning character of His death? He claimed to die as a Priest, to lay down His life of His own free will for the world's iniquity. How could He have dared to offer a stained life as a sacrifice for stained lives? The judge of souls and the atoner for souls must, in virtue of these very claims, be sinless.

2. His character is a positive as well as a negative exhibition of goodness. His sinlessness means that He was full of love to God and man, and that that perfect love expressed itself completely. The difficulty which the human imagination finds in describing a perfect character is in making it positive. It is comparatively easy to avoid introducing faults; the difficulty is to represent virtues. The character of Jesus is faultless, but not exhibited like the faultless characters of the human imagination, but, on the contrary, full of positiveness, freshness, and force.

3. His character is marked by the balance as well as the perfection of excellence. Great virtues are nearly akin to vices, and in men we never find the balance preserved. Dignity passes easily into pride, reflection into coldness, sincerity into bluntness, civility into insincerity — in short, a finite nature exhausts itself by efforts in a temporary direction. But in Christ there is no want of balance. The character is one faultless in its perfection. Attention has been called to the balance He observes between severity and tenderness. None denounces evil with such terrible force. The generation in which He lives is adulterous, evil, sinful, wicked, perverse. And yet He is profoundly tender along with it all. He weeps over doomed Jerusalem, defends the condemned adulteress against her accusers, and absolves the sinful woman who bathes His feet with her tears. Something might also be said of the balance He keeps between manliness and womanliness. "The character we call manly," it has been said with some truth, "is

not the normal type. We have had such struggles with barbarism, and courage and firmness have been so useful, that we have come to regard them as distinctive of man, while in fact they are only distinctive of *fallen* man."[1] His character is winning, and His power of drawing affection, as well as His power of enduring suffering, are feminine. But there is no weakness in it all.

4. His character is perfectly simple. He makes no attempt to dazzle or startle. He has none of the eccentricities of genius. His mode of life, His dress, His habits, are without a trace of pretension. His life is all of one piece—the most wonderful events and the most ordinary. He works a miracle, takes a meal, speaks an imperishable parable, all as they come, living His life quietly from hour to hour. Simplicity is a mark of greatness; none was ever so perfectly simple as He.

5. He lays great stress upon hitherto unrecognised virtues. Coming into the world at a time when force was worshipped as virtue itself, He made much of the passive virtues, and showed that to suffer well was at least as much as to act well. When Peter commends His example, He lays special emphasis on this: "Who, when He was reviled, reviled not again; when He suffered, He threatened not; but committed Himself to Him who judgeth righteously." Patience, humility, meekness—these were restored by Him to their forgotten but true place. We are forbidden to

[1] George Steward, *Memoirs*, p. 97.

select any virtues as specially characterising Him, for in Him all the virtues met in supreme excellence and perfect harmony. But we may note the prominence He gave to these.

He left us an example. "Always and everywhere have Him devoutly before the eyes of your mind—in His behaviour and in His ways, as when He is with His disciples and when He is with sinners, when He speaks and when He preaches, when He goes forth and when He sits down, when He sleeps and when He wakes, when He eats and when He serves others, when He heals the sick and when He does His other miracles, setting forth to thyself and thy heart His ways and His doings, how humbly He bore Himself among men, how tenderly among His disciples; how pitiful He was to the poor, to whom He made Himself like in all things, and who seemed to be His own special family; how He despised none or shrank from them, not even from the leper; how He paid no court to the rich; how free He was from the cares of the world, and from trouble about the needs of the body; how patient under insult, and how gentle in answering, for He sought not to maintain His cause by keen and bitter words, but with gentle and humble answer to cure another's malice; what composure in all His behaviour, what anxiety for the salvation of souls, for the love of whom He also deigned to die; how He offered Himself as the pattern of all that is good; how compassionate He was to the afflicted; how He condescended to the imperfection of the weak, how He despised not success, how mercifully He received the penitent, how dutiful He was to His parents; how ready in serving all, according to His own words, 'I am among you as He that doth serve'; how He shunned all display and show, all singularity; how He avoided all occasions of offence, how temperate in eating and drinking, how modest in appearance, how earnest in prayer, how sober in His watching, how patient of toil and want, how peaceful and calm in all things."[1]

This is Christ as an example, and if He be allowed to be the perfect example, the ideal of humanity, the flower and crown of the creation, the region of the miraculous has been entered. A sinless man is a violation of the natural order. But besides that, there is clearly traceable in the character itself a divine element, which calls for worship on our part, as well as for imitation. He is not simply a perfect man, and those who saw Him did not build on His perfection, which they took for granted, but upon His works. He is not to be analysed as Paul, though Paul seems nearer to Christ than we do to Paul. Between Paul and Christ there is a space which we cannot measure; and the comparison of the Saviour, even with His greatest apostle, makes us cry, "My Lord and my God."

This impression produced on those who knew Him —the impression of a character by no means exhausted when it was pronounced sinless—is confirmed when we analyse particular virtues. He does not show the ordinary lawful human emotions. He does not think

[1] Rudolphus de Saxonia, quoted in F. Coleridge's *Vita vitæ nostræ*, and Church's *Human Life*, p. 192.

of Himself at all; He had no self-interest. He does not seek to justify Himself. When He is awakened in the storm, He exhibits no emotion of human terror. When He stands before unjust judges, He utters no words of natural wrath. When He withdraws Himself from those who are ready to stone Him, it is not a timid man crouching behind the pillars of the temple, but one who wields superhuman power, passing with the majesty of God through His enemies.[1] When He describes Himself as meek and lowly in heart, He makes these words the groundwork of an invitation for weary and sin-laden souls to come to Him. He does not ask for favours, nor show gratitude for them when they are received. These are works that are due to Him. He is conscious of Kingship, Messiahship, miraculous power, but has nothing of what we all call self-respect. It is all power and no pride.

Is not all this the idea of God? And we close by repeating the question of the beginning, " Whence came He? how is He to be accounted for?" Jesus Christ must be accounted for. He is the problem of this age especially, and He will be the problem of all the ages. What account of Christ will stand? Was He dreamed into being? Then the dreamer must be equal to the man he dreamed. Those who make this reply, must, it has been well said, account for the man born in the imagination of some other man, who, as a creature of imagination, has risen to the supreme place in human history, and who to-day rules millions of human lives and destinies. For this is the wonderful thing about His character, that He has been the con-

[1] See Aquinas, *Summa*, xliii. 3.

stant standard of all the different ages. The best idea of each age has been embodied in Him. He was seen at first as the great Prophet and Teacher of mankind, then as the ideal of a life of self-devoted poverty, then as a great improver and reformer, then as the example of humanity—all true ideas, but none complete. Each age has been touched and swayed by Him, but He is always above and before the ages, and still as they go they find Him answering to their best thoughts and hopes. As it has been, so it will be; that model will ever rise above the greatest thoughts of men, and the greatest things even that have been said and thought about itself. The generations may make great advances, and find much that their predecessors have never thought or cared for; but however great their advances may be, that same figure will continue to lead their march.

NOTES

Note A.—The Descent into Egypt

This suggestion was originally made in the *Expositor* by the Rev. W. G. Elmslie, who connects it with the sojourn of Israel in Egypt.

Note B.—The Baptism

On this subject compare Owen, *Discourse concerning the Holy Spirit*, book ii. ch. 4. Owen admits that Christ "was probably acted by the Spirit in and unto many extraordinary actions during His career of a private life, but the fulness of gifts for His work He received not until the time of His baptism."

Note C.—The Temptation

Compare on this subject the *Quarterly Review*, 1874, in a review of Farrar's *Life of Christ;* also a very suggestive sermon by Dr. Maclaren in the *Sunday at Home*, 1880. The significance of the temptation to Christ is perhaps nowhere more profoundly treated than in Mr. Maurice's Sermons on the Temptation.

NOTE D.—THE MIRACLE AT CANA

A striking sermon on this subject will be found in Mozley's *Sermons: Parochial and Occasional.* The view of the words, " Mine hour is not yet come," given in the text, is substantially that presented in the *Expositor* by Rev. Rayner Winterbotham. Dr. W. G. Ward's essay, previously referred to, is instructive.

NOTE E.—THE RESURRECTION

" This presentiment of a resurrection . . . is too feeble very materially and immediately to lighten Job's sorrows. The momentary gleam is swallowed up by the closing darkness, and the benighted wanderer's blindness seems intenser from the supernatural glare of the light that for a moment filled his eye."—A. B. DAVIDSON, *A Commentary on Job,* Introduction, p. 31.

NOTE F.—THE RESURRECTION LIFE

The view taken throughout the chapter is that of Canon Westcott in the singularly profound essay he contributed to the *Contemporary Review,* vol. xxx. The subject is carefully treated by Dr. E. Robinson in the *Bibliotheca Sacra,* 1845. Compare also *The Risen Lord's Interdict on Mary,* by S. D. F. Salmond; *The Resurrection of Christ,* by R. W. Macan.

WORKS BY W. ROBERTSON NICOLL.

THE LAMB OF GOD. Third Edition. 2s. 6d.

THE KEY OF THE GRAVE. Fourth Edition. 3s. 6d.

SONGS OF REST. Second Edition. 5s.

TEN-MINUTE SERMONS. Fourth Edition. 3s. 6d.

THE SEVEN WORDS FROM THE CROSS. Second Edition. 1s. 6d.

WORKS BEARING ON THE
LIFE AND PERSON OF CHRIST,
PUBLISHED BY
T. & T. CLARK, 38 GEORGE STREET, EDINBURGH.

Andrews (Rev. S. J.)—The Life of Our Lord upon the Earth: Considered in its Historical, Chronological, and Geographical Relations. New Edition, thoroughly revised. The only Authorised Edition in this country. Demy 8vo, 9s.

Bruce (A. B., D.D.)—The Kingdom of God; or, Christ's Teaching according to the Synoptical Gospels. Sixth Edition, post 8vo, 7s. 6d.
'A remarkable book.'—*Saturday Review.*

Bruce (A. B., D.D.)—The Training of the Twelve. Fifth Edition, 8vo, 10s. 6d.
'A volume which can never lose its charm either for the preacher or for the ordinary Christian reader.'—*London Quarterly Review.*

Bruce (A. B., D.D.)—The Humiliation of Christ. Fourth Edition, 8vo, 10s. 6d.
'This noble theological treatise.'—*Evangelical Magazine.*

Caspari (C. E.)—A Chronological and Geographical Introduction to THE LIFE OF CHRIST. 8vo, 7s. 6d.
'No Bible student should fail to make this treatise his constant friend and companion.'—*Bell's Weekly Messenger.*

Caspers (A.)—The Footsteps of Christ. Crown 8vo, 7s. 6d.

Dorner (Professor)—History of the Development of the Doctrine of THE PERSON OF CHRIST. Five vols. 8vo, £2, 12s. 6d.

Ebrard (Dr. J. H. A.)—The Gospel History: A Compendium of Critical Investigations in support of the Four Gospels. 8vo, 10s. 6d.

Hall (Rev. Newman, D.D.)—The Lord's Prayer: A Practical Meditation. Second Edition, crown 8vo, 4s. 6d.
'The author's thoughts are sharply cut, and are like crystals in their clearness and power.'—*British Quarterly Review.*

Hall (Rev. Newman, D.D.)—Gethsemane: Leaves of Healing from the Garden of Grief. Crown 8vo, 4s.
'Richly laden with consolation for the afflicted children of God; and from the first page to the last it does not strike one false note.'—*Christian Leader.*

Krummacher (Dr. F. W.)—The Suffering Saviour. Crown 8vo, 7s. 6d.
'To the devout and earnest Christian the volume will be a treasure indeed.'—*Wesleyan Times.*

Lange (J. P., D.D.)—The Life of Our Lord Jesus Christ. Edited, with additional Notes, by Prof. MARCUS DODS, D.D. Second Edition, in Four vols. 8vo, Subscription price, 28s.

Lehmann (Pastor E.)—Scenes from the Life of Jesus. Cr. 8vo, 3s. 6d.
'There is in these lectures a tender sympathy, and a spiritual devoutness and simplicity, which gives to them a real charm.'—*Literary World.*

Lilley (J. P., B.D.)—The Lord's Supper: Its Origin, Nature, and Use. Crown 8vo, 5s.
'We know no better modern book more suggestive and helpful.'—*Freeman.*

[*Continued on next page.*

Naville (Ernest)—The Christ. Seven Lectures. Translated by Rev.
T. J. DESPRÉS. Crown 8vo, 4s. 6d.
'Ministers who wish for suggestions and guidance as to the manner in which they can treat of the pressingly important subject which is considered by M. Naville, should take pains to acquaint themselves with this volume.'—*Christian World.*

Nicoll (W. R., LL.D.)—The Incarnate Saviour: A Life of Jesus Christ. New Edition, crown 8vo, 3s. 6d.
'It commands my warm sympathy and admiration.'—*Canon Liddon.*

Ross (C., M.A.)—Our Father's Kingdom: Lectures on the Lord's Prayer. Crown 8vo, 2s. 6d.

Salmond (Professor)—The Life of Christ. Bible Class Primers. Paper covers, 6d.; cloth, 8d.
'A scholarly and beautiful presentation of the story of the Four Gospels.'—*Sunday School Chronicle.*

Scrymgeour (Wm.)—Lessons on the Life of Christ. Bible Class Handbooks, 2s. 6d.
'A thoroughly satisfactory help to teacher and scholar.'—*British Messenger.*

Stalker (Jas., D.D.)—A Life of Christ. Bible Class Handbooks. Crown 8vo, 1s. 6d.; large type Edition, handsomely bound, 3s. 6d.
'As a succinct, suggestive, beautifully written exhibition of the life of our Lord, we are acquainted with nothing that can compare with it.'—*Christian World.*

Steinmeyer (Dr. F. L.)—The Miracles of Our Lord: Examined in their relation to Modern Criticism. 8vo, 7s. 6d.
'Will take its place among the best recent volumes of Christian evidence.'—*Standard.*

Steinmeyer (Dr. F. L.)—The History of the Passion and Resurrection OF OUR LORD, in the Light of Modern Criticism. 8vo, 10s. 6d.
'Will well repay earnest study.'—*Weekly Review.*

Stier (Dr. Rudolph)—On the Words of the Lord Jesus. Eight vols. 8vo (or the Eight vols. bound in FOUR), £2, 2s. *net.* Separate volumes may be had, price 10s. 6d.
'The whole work is a treasury of thoughtful exposition.'—*Guardian.*

Ullmann (Dr. Carl)—The Sinlessness of Jesus: An Evidence for Christianity. Third Edition, crown 8vo, 6s.
'Ullmann has studied the sinlessness of Christ more profoundly, and written on it more beautifully, than any other theologian.'—FARRAR'S *Life of Christ.*

Weiss (Dr. Bernhard)—The Life of Christ. Three vols. 8vo, 31s. 6d.
'From the thoroughness of the discussion and clearness of the writer, we anticipate a very valuable addition to the Great Biography.'—*Freeman.*

Wendt (Prof. H. H.)—The Teaching of Jesus. Two vols. 8vo, 21s.
'A brilliant and satisfactory exposition of the teaching of Christ.'—*Expositor.*

The Voice from the Cross: A Series of Sermons on Our Lord's Passion by eminent Living Preachers of Germany. Edited and translated by WM. MACINTOSH, M.A., F.S.S. Crown 8vo, 5s.
'Is certain to be welcomed with devout gratitude by every evangelical Christian in Britain.'—*Christian Leader.*

T. & T. Clark's Publications.

HANDBOOKS FOR BIBLE CLASSES AND PRIVATE STUDENTS.

EDITED BY

PROF. MARCUS DODS, D.D., AND ALEXANDER WHYTE, D.D.

'I name specially the admirable Handbooks for Bible Classes issued by T. & T. Clark of Edinburgh. They are very cheap, and among them are some books unsurpassed in their kind.'—Dr. W. ROBERTSON NICOLL in *The British Weekly.*

COMMENTARIES—

Professor MARCUS DODS, D.D. **Genesis.** 2s.
JAMES MACGREGOR, D.D. **Exodus.** 2 Vols. 2s. each.
Principal DOUGLAS, D.D. **Joshua.** 1s. 6d.
Professor J. G. MURPHY, LL.D. **Chronicles.** 1s. 6d.
Professor MARCUS DODS, D.D. **Haggai, Zechariah, Malachi.** 2s.
Principal DOUGLAS, D.D. **Obadiah to Zephaniah.** 1s. 6d.
Professor T. M. LINDSAY, D.D. **Mark.** 2s. 6d.

Professor T. M. LINDSAY, D.D. **St. Luke.** 2 Vols. 3s. 3d. (Vol. I., 2s.; Vol. II., 1s. 3d.).
GEORGE REITH, D.D. **St. John.** 2 Vols. 2s. each.
Professor T. M. LINDSAY, D.D. **Acts.** 2 Vols. 1s. 6d. each.
Principal BROWN, D.D. **Romans.** 2s.
JAMES MACGREGOR, D.D. **Galatians.** 1s. 6d.
Professor J. S. CANDLISH, D.D. **Ephesians.** 1s. 6d.
Professor A. B. DAVIDSON, D.D. **Hebrews.** 2s. 6d.

GENERAL SUBJECTS—

JAMES STALKER, D.K.
    The Life of Christ. 1s. 6d.
    The Life of St. Paul. 1s. 6d.
    (*Large-type Editions,* 3s. 6d. each.)
ALEXANDER WHYTE, D.D.
    The Shorter Catechism. 2s. 6d.
Professor J. S. CANDLISH, D.D.
    The Christian Sacraments. 1s. 6d.
    The Christian Doctrine of God. 1s. 6d.
    The Work of the Holy Spirit. 1s. 6d.
    The Biblical Doctrine of Sin. 1s. 6d.
NORMAN L. WALKER, D.D.
    Scottish Church History. 1s. 6d.
Rev. W. D. THOMSON, M.A.
    The Christian Miracles and the Conclusions of Science. 2s.
GEORGE SMITH, LL.D., F.R.G.S., C.I.E.
    History of Christian Missions. 2s. 6d.
ARCHIBALD HENDERSON, D.D.
    Palestine: Its Historical Geography. *With Maps.* 2s. 6d.
Professor T. M. LINDSAY, D.D.
    The Reformation. 2s.

Rev. JOHN MACPHERSON, M.A.
    The Sum of Saving Knowledge. 1s. 6d.
    The Confession of Faith. 2s.
    Presbyterianism. 1s. 6d.
Professor BINNIE, D.D.
    The Church. 1s. 6d.
Rev. T. B. KILPATRICK, B.D.
    Butler's Three Sermons on Human Nature. 1s. 6d.
President HAMILTON, D.D.
    History of the Irish Presbyterian Church. 2s.
Rev. W. SCRYMGEOUR, M.A.
    Lessons on the Life of Christ. 2s. 6d.
A. TAYLOR INNES, M.A., Advocate.
    Church and State. 3s.
Rev. J. FEATHER.
    The Last of the Prophets—John the Baptist. 2s.
Rev. W. FAIRWEATHER, M.A.
    From the Exile to the Advent. 2s.
Professor J. LAIDLAW, D.D.
    Foundation Truths of Scripture as to Sin and Salvation. 1s. 6d.
Rev. L. A. MUIRHEAD, B.D.
    The Times of Christ. 2s.

www.ingramcontent.com/pod-product-compliance
Lightning Source LLC
Chambersburg PA
CBHW021212240426
43667CB00038B/360